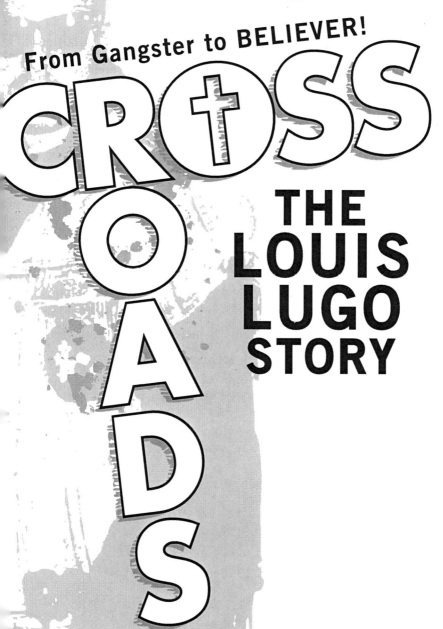

From Gangster to BELIEVER!

CR✝SS
O
A
D
S

THE LOUIS LUGO STORY

R.S. HUNTER

"A Sobering Read" - Rev. Victor Maldonado

Crossroads: The Louis Lugo Story © 2011 Reverend Louis Lugo
Cover design by Erik Evec
Edited by Ron D. Mead

References: Louis Lugo, King James (KJ) Bible and English
Standard Version (ESV) Bible.

All of the situations or events depicted are true, and the details
within this story are based on actual events. Some names have been
changed to protect their identity.

An Amethyst Moon Book
Published by AMETHYST MOON PUBLISHING
P.O. Box 87885
Tucson, AZ 85754
www.ampubbooks.com

ISBN 978-1-935354-60-4 (13 digit)
1-935354-60-4 (10 digit)

· Library of Congress Control Number: 2011937371

I dedicate this book to:

- *To God*
- *My wife Regina*
- *My children Louis, Tiffany, Crystal, and Antonio*
- *Victor Maldonado, who didn't give up on me*
- *The victims of the streets*

--Reverend L.A. Lugo

Contents

Foreword

The Reverend Louis Lugo once said, "You ain't going to believe some of the stuff I have to tell you. Looking back, I can't believe it myself. How can someone who has danced upon the edge for so many decades still be here today to talk about it? You name it—I've done it! Did I care about who I was hurting? No! That wasn't part of the rules I lived by. My standard was the standard of survival, on the streets, doing whatever I had to do to stay on top. There was no pride in being anywhere else. It was either rule or be ruled. I always ruled!"

Crossroads is the true to life story of a young boy's journey, directly into Hell. There were no other options available to him. He suffered at the abusive hands of others, so it wasn't surprising to see how his survival skills evolved. Not even ten years old yet, but this skinny little Puerto Rican kid was already a force to be reckoned with. Respect his space or fall victim to his wrath—a wrath equal to the disciplines he would constantly endure.

There is a bright side to this tale of woe, a miracle, if you will. If you look at the statistics of how many kids living within the poorest neighborhoods of our cities end up being beaten down by the very system that is in place to protect them, the numbers are staggering. Will a convicted felon ever get a fighting chance to improve his or her station in life? Not likely! Louie Lugo not only beat the odds, he shattered them. Drugs, prostitution, crimes of

10 violence, and multiple convictions all had a part in evolving this man into the God-fearing, spiritual-serving warrior he is today. You would think that being shot and stabbed multiple times would have killed him or at least broken his spirit. No, not this guy. Instead, it all became an intricate part of a mission, a ministry, a story. God was about to use him in ways Louie could never have imagined. The Bible mentions countless stories of where God used someone undesirable for His own will. Was Louis a modern day Paul or a thief hanging upon the cross? In some very special ways, yes he was! It is because of where Louie comes from and the path that was his life, that his sermons have such a powerful punch. If God can use Louie in the battlefield today, just think of how He can use you—if you let Him.

This is the story that will expose you to the Devil's deadly grip. It can be broken. It must be broken. Allow Reverend Louis Lugo to walk you through the paths that lead him to where he is today You will stand at the crossroads with him, thinking he should turn right, only to see him turn left. He will pay dearly for his wrong decisions. He will pay in blood. But as you will see, Louie finally makes it back onto the right path, leaving the crossroads to slowly fade behind him. May you be blessed as you read each and every page. May your spark ignite the fire so that others may see Welcome to *Crossroads—The Louis Lugo Story.*

A True Story…

Chapter 1: You Don't Know Them Like I Do

The itching was unbearable as he brought his disposable lighter to life. The flickering flame danced as the surrounding darkness slowly gave way to the eerie glow. A mixture of soft white powder and a few drops of water waited patiently for the soothing of the heat. The bottom of the spoon was blackened as it sucked every bit of energy it could from the flame. The mixture started to boil violently for a brief moment. The time was at hand for the cares of the world to go away, at least for a short time. The needle's tip poked into the center of the poisonous puddle as his trembling hand worked the plunger. The spoon was now clean; its contents magically absorbed into the syringe. With a scarf tightly pulled against what used to be considered a bicep, his pitifully dying vein struggled to pop into view—waiting, begging, needing. The needle fought with the callous outer layers of his skin but soon found its mark: his body's lifeline to the heart and brain. As he pulled the plunger slightly back, his blood entered the syringe morphing with the fix before all of the contents quickly disappeared. It was done. With a quick release of the scarf and the retraction of the needle, the sensations started to take over every fiber of his body. His vomit came immediately, but that was expected. Vomit always equaled ecstasy.

It was the wrenching sound of the junkie's purging that usually woke me from this nightmarish dream. This nightmare was a

14   familiar one: one of the worst. I would lie there soaked in sweat contemplating who I used to be. I am the man who sold this junkie his fix. To him I was a hero. To me, it was simply a job. His short lived life was my haunting ghost. As I look back at who I used to be, I now realize that I was simply one of the Devil's many minions. He had me so deep in a hole that I never imagined finding a way out. But I did. Today, I am a new man, by the grace of God. My name is Reverend Louis Lugo, and this is my story. I don't have those nightmares very often now, but they are still there, itching to be released.

Although my struggle with the dark side is constant and unyielding, I thank God for my strength. I am winning the tug-of-war. My most recent battle was not that long ago. I remember that day like it was yesterday. The smell of freshly brewed coffee filled the cool November air, kids running around excited about the beginning of a new day, a special day. I could hear the bacon crackling in the pan, being prepared just the way I liked it, extra crispy. I knew the eggs were almost ready. The sounds and smells were lifting my spirits. "Praise God," I whispered as I made my way to the kitchen, excited about what was waiting for me there. My family gathered to share this Sunday morning feast. I was truly blessed and not just for this meal. After giving thanks for the food, I smiled as I pondered what the day had in store for me. I was excited and nervous, all at the same time.

Preston Moore was not only the White Hall fire chief but also the one who invited me to speak at the Perry Chapel Baptist Church in Warsaw, Ohio. During the Ohio Martial Arts tournaments, Preston was the onsite fireman in charge of the first aid programs affiliated with the *Ohio Martial Arts Magazine* (our magazine—

our pride and joy). I had to make a difficult decision that weekend. *15*
If I accepted the invite to speak to an entire congregation, I would
have to miss the two-day martial arts tournament being held the
same weekend. The Devil was in full attack mode. My choices
were limited, my options few.

Knowing that I was a diabetic, the evil one knew that I was not
in any condition to manage the responsibilities of the tournament
plus drive all the way to Warsaw for my presentation. The recovery
from a two-day tournament usually involved at least two days of
rest. Working three days in a row just wasn't an option. The Devil
tried to convince me that I should stay focused on the tournament
and turn down the invitation to speak at the Perry Chapel Baptist
Church; he reminded me that I would not be able to handle the
fatigue I would experience afterwards. Staying home was the only
option he gave me. I prayed hard. The Devil was right: there really
was only one choice, so I didn't hesitate for a moment. I accepted
the speaking engagement in Warsaw. I had a story to tell, and I
needed it to land upon as many ears as possible.

I felt like I had a debt to repay—I owed the Baptists big time,
and I was one who always paid my debts. Even though I was raised
in a Pentecostal church, I never thought of myself as a Baptist. I
was invited by my cousin Pe Pe to attend the 53rd annual Baptist
revival being held at the Tabernacle Baptist Church in Columbus,
Ohio. This week-long event was almost over when I finally found
some spare time and decided to show up. The day I arrived, April
, 2004, was the last day of the revival. I entered it not knowing
exactly what the Baptists had to offer me. I assumed I would walk
out of there the same person I was when I entered. I was never
so wrong. You see, being baptized in water is a tradition in the

16 church, regardless if you are dunked or sprinkled. It is a symbol of being renewed or reborn. When I heard Reverend Nathaniel Johnson speak that day, I was totally baptized in the Word.

I indeed have baptized you with water: but he shall baptize you with the Holy Ghost. (Mark 1:18)

Those words proved to be so true. From that day on, I felt that I owed the Baptist my life. I was indebted to the Baptist community. When Preston Moore invited me to Warsaw, I was now able to pay back these spiritual warriors. The Devil was telling me to ignore the invitation, not to waste my time. "Aren't you a diabetic? You'll never make it" was constantly being whispered into my ear by one of his many minions working me over. The more they taunted me, the stronger my resolve became. Genesis 4:7 started repeating in my mind.

If you do what is right, will you not be accepted? But if you do not do what is right, sin is crouching at your door; it desires you, you must master it.

My accepting this offer in Warsaw was the only option I dared consider—my way of mastering my own sin. I needed to tell my truth, the ugly truth. I knew this was God's will, so it was my pleasure to follow blindly. As I showered, I pondered what the day had in store for me. I smiled to myself knowing that God's will for me was perfect in every way. I had tried conforming to the dark side of this world for so many years, and it brought me nothing but grief and sorrow. With my renewed spirit, I knew it was God' will for me to drive to Warsaw. I didn't realize it at the time that the Devil and his army was going to taunt and tease me every step of the way.

I assumed that this would be a family outing, something we could share together—wrong! Although my wife was eager to spend the day with me, my kids had another plan, one that didn't include spending an hour-and-a half driving each way to and from Warsaw. They had their minds made up, reassuring me that they had heard my sermon many times before and probably could repeat it, verbatim. To keep the peace, my wife suggested that I make the drive myself, and she would take the kids to our regular church.

This Sunday was indeed a special day. Yes, I had the usual blessings of waking up to a house full of wonderful smells and sounds. People who loved me surrounded me within my world, and for that I am always amazed. But today was different. I had a certain vigor to my step as I started preparing for the path that God had placed before me. Even though I was tired and my body ached from working the past two days, I reflected upon Psalms 18:32:

It is God that girdeth me with strength,
and maketh my way perfect.

That verse helped me set my priorities straight. I was focused on the day and the moment. A certain glow of contentment was beaming from my smile. Okay, I understand why my kids wanted to stay behind, and I appreciated the sacrifice my wife made in staying with them. I would be making the trip by myself. An hour-and-a half is a wonderful amount of time to spend alone with God. He and I would talk during the entire drive. Actually, He talked while I listened. Of course, the Devil would try to join in the conversation; I had to fight hard to keep him at bay.

As I approached Warsaw and continued following my carefully noted directions, I found myself amazed at the surroundings, at the intense beauty of the cornfields and manicured lawns. The trees hovered overhead like the wings of angels. I knew I was entering God's country. God was blessing me, and I was absorbing it all. As I approached the church, I noticed a small parking lot up ahead, right next to a small church. *How quaint*, I thought as I parked as far from the building as I could. I wanted to take it all in as I walked to the church's entrance.

To my surprise, as I approached the far end of the parking lot, I found two more parking lots, completely packed with cars. I pondered out loud, "How on earth could all these people fit into that small building?" God showed me the answer immediately. A young couple approached me and must have overheard my comments. They laughed as they led me up towards the chapel. Behind that cute little church, which from a distance looked perfect in every way, sat a much larger, newer worship center. Now I knew were all the people were. I was speechless, stunned, and scared. Then the Devil saw his opportunity. He saw my fear and started taking advantage of that weakness. If you leave the door to your soul slightly open, the Devil will find a way to come on in, uninvited. He had me convinced that I wasn't supposed to be there. After all, these were extremely spiritual people who could probably quote scripture as perfectly as it was written. What would a gangster like me have to say to these folks? Why would they even be interested in listening to what I had to say? The Devil was filling my mind with these and other doubting questions, and my mind was floating in them. The Devil was convincing me that I couldn't handle this. He wasn't asking me to leave; he was telling me, loud and clear, to get out of there, now! He was pretending that he knew what was best for me and that he cared. I was just about to turn around and run back to the safety of my car when Preston Moore opened the door, saw me, and said with a smile, "Oh, I am so glad you made it. Are you ready for this?"

His voice was calming and reassuring as he led me into the rear of the worship center, backstage, behind the pulpit. I followed, keeping one eye on my escape, just in case the Devil won the day. Praise God, he didn't!

I was reminded of the story in Joshua where it talks about Rahab the harlot and the spies. When Joshua sent two spies to Jericho, Rahab protected them by lying to the king. The spies told her that because of her kindness, she would be saved when the city is taken. When they promised her that the Lord would spare her house, she asked about her brothers, sisters, mother, and father. She was told that all the people she brings into her house would be saved, and they were. Here I was battling Satan as I approached this church, God's house, and as with Rahab's family, once I was brought into His house, I felt safe. The Devil couldn't touch me here. My fears soon faded, but I still had questions—I was curious. As I reflected on how God used Rahab, I smiled realizing that if He could use her, a prostitute, then it made sense why He would use a hustler like me.

While sitting behind the pulpit, waiting to be introduced, I was deep in prayer, speaking with God, trying to understand it all. Preston came to check up on me and could see that I was a little nervous. I never spoke to a congregation like this before. Usually my speaking engagements were more in the classroom setting where I would sit and talk to kids, want-a-be gangsters, and educate them on where their path was taking them. However, this situation was different: people—mature, responsible spiritual folks—were eagerly waiting to hear what this bum had to say. I was in awe, and

I let God know it. Preston simply said, "Just tell them your story. Speak about your magazine's mission, and everything will work out just fine."

Preston's words were reassuring as I smiled back at him. He quickly disappeared again, off to take care of other behind-the-scene details.

As the organist played, I was lost in my own world, with just God and me. All the noise around me faded as did the light. I was now in a quiet place, with God and me, conversing. I asked God one more time to guide my mouth so that the words I was about to speak would be His, not mine. Within a few brief moments of time, I contemplated the journey that was my life and how it led to this day, this church, and this chair hidden behind this pulpit. I looked up and asked in a whisper, "Why me God? Why did you select me to speak to these people? Why have you placed me here, today, to speak to the masses?"

God answered me in such a way it almost knocked me to my knees. I now knew without any doubt that I was following His illuminated path. He shouted these words, "You don't know them like I do!"

I was humbled to the point of tears. While those words echoed within my head, God took my hand and started showing me my life, starting at the moment of my birth. God was answering my question, in ugly, horrid, bloody detail. This was to be my story and I knew it like the back of my hand. God wanted to remind me of who I was and how I came to be sitting on this chair, behind this pulpit, in this church. This is what He showed me; this is what I saw.

The year was 1958 and as the ninth of September rolled around,

Aida, my mother, was ready for me to come into this world to stop causing her such a backache. She was admitted to the birthing center at the Saint Mary's Hospital on the corner of St. Marks and Buffalo, right in the heart of Brooklyn's notorious Bedford Stuyvesant, Kingsborough. Kingsborough was the type of place that you read about in thriller novels or saw in gangster movies. The projects were so corrupt that when the sun went down, even the cops would stay away. The gangs ruled the streets, my streets. This was my home, the neighborhood that would sculpt my young mind into the man I became. The streets would become my classroom, and I would prove to be an "A" student to its lessons. It was simply a matter of survival, and I survived. Others perished!

My birth was uneventful, and shortly after my mother was able to leave the hospital, I was brought back to our home, a tiny two bedroom apartment on Saint John's Street. I shared my cramped living space with my two sisters, Iris and Madeline, and with my mom and dad. My father's abuses towards my mom not only hurt her but also trickled down into the fiber of all who lived under his roof. He didn't even have the common decency to show up for my birth, which I guess, in retrospect, was a good thing. His toys and carts were more important to him than family, blood.

When I was about one year old, we moved to Puerto Rico to try to start a new life. We stayed with my father's mother Mymysala in her small, primitive house without running water. Having to use an outhouse was as luxurious as it got. This arrangement lasted only two years before we moved back to Brownsville on Saratoga Avenue, Brooklyn.

Now three years old, I was starting to develop into the person would become, influenced by those around me: my sisters, my aunts, my mother, and yes, even my father. When I reached the age of four, I was speaking broken English with a heavy Spanish accent. I had a lot of difficulty communicating, although those close to me seemed to understand what I was trying to say. These were good years with happy memories. I can recall my sister Madeline's birthday; Iris and I pooled our savings to purchase a toy tea set as a birthday gift. Even though we were a few dollars short, the store clerk appreciated the attempt we were making and sold us the toy for exactly what we had in pocket change, tax included. Iris and I were so pleased with ourselves. Madeline was surprised, and Mom was proud. As I grew up, I developed a strong family bond, not only with my sisters, grandmother, aunts, and mother, but with what I would refer to as my adopted brothers from downstairs—Croc, Cheddar, Skull, Big D, and Racket. Everyone was known by their street name. I hadn't earned mine yet. We would look out for each other, and as I started growing and becoming one with the street, I was glad to have them by my side.

When I was five years old, we moved once again, this time to Park Place in Crown Heights. I missed the Kingsborough Projects and would often make the solo trip back to the hood to hang with my brothers. Since my aunts and grandma still lived there, it seemed like I had the perfect excuse for wandering the streets alone. Still my mom would get angry at me. She didn't think I was old enough to travel the mile or so from one neighborhood to another. Her reasoning was that it was unsafe for me to cross so many streets. "But Mom, I look both ways before crossing," I would assure her but to no avail. In Mom's defense, I was only five; she had a valid point. I still preferred to deal with Mom's wrath in exchange for being able to visit Croc and my other brothers. Croc and I were th same age and had a lot in common—fighting.

Being a smaller kid, I did have my share of problems within the school system. I attended P.S. 141 on Park Place, a primarily black school. Since I looked white, it was assumed that I was an easy target, that is, until they made the mistake of getting in my face. Usually Croc was there to help me with the fights, to even the score, so I was grateful for that. I watched him and learned real fast. The lessons of the street were beginning, and I was a quick study. When Croc wasn't around, I had to put my learning to the test. I fought often; I fought hard. I won some and sometimes I lost, but more importantly, I gained a valuable reputation. It seems that this short Spanish kid from Puerto Rico wasn't such an easy target after all.

Racism was a big problem, and someone like me was a target from both the black and white kids. I had it coming from all directions. They knew that picking on me one-on-one was a losing proposition. Their tactics evolved into more ambushes, taking me by surprise—two, three or more jumping on me at the same time. All I could do was curl up, protect myself, take whatever they gave me, and know that my day would come. After experiencing a beat down, I would make my way back home to my brothers. When Croc would hear what happened, he would go into revenge mode. We would go hunting for those who assaulted me. It was time for payback! We showed no mercy; the justice was swift and severe.

This was also the year when I experienced one of my happiest days; we moved back to Kingsborough, back to my family, and back to my streets. Just before we moved, my father got into another one of his abusive, drunken moods. This time it was different; he had a strange look in his eyes, a look I will never forget. That crazy bastard grabbed my mother, spun her around, and put a knife to her throat while yelling "trash" at her and at us. This wasn't the first time he tried this. He held her in front of us pressing the sharp blade tightly against her skin. "Say goodbye to your mother," he raged. My mother, fearing for her life, thinking that this time he would actually do it, screamed out a pitiful mourn, "Oh God help me. Please help me. He's going to kill me in front of my children!"

Her pleading prayer must have really shocked my dad. Realizing what he was doing and being snapped back into a brief moment of sanity, he dropped the knife while releasing his tight grip on her. Something changed in my father that day. I like to think that God heard my mother's plea and decided to give my father a mighty spiritual smack, right upside the head.

Hebrews 4:12

For the word of God is living and active, sharper than any two-edged sword, piercing to the division of soul and of spirit, of joints and of marrow, and discerning the thoughts and intentions of the heart.

Chapter 2: A Quarter Goes a Long Way

Being independent minded and eager to explore, I continued to travel around the hood at an extremely young age. From my point of view, I was simply coming of age, discovering all that needed to be discovered, with total disregard of the consequences. I'd been cruising these streets for over three years now, and contrary to what my mother thought, I wasn't going to get run over by a speeding car while trying to cross busy intersections. I wasn't about to get lost. I wasn't going to be kidnapped by some sex-craved maniac or ax murderer, never to be seen by my family again. Actually, I felt safer on these streets than I did anywhere else. People knew that if they messed with me, they were messing with five others, all capable of doing serious harm. I was not afraid!

I loved to travel to the Fort Green Projects, sometimes with Croc but mostly by myself. This is where I would get to see my uncles, including my adoptive uncle, Nicky Cruz (the biggest, toughest dude there ever was). I never had to worry about anything when I was near Uncle Nicky. Nobody messed with any of us. Nicky, being the president of the Mau Maus, was respected for his insight and fairness but was also known for his willingness to fight anyone, big or small, young or old, anywhere, anytime. I never really understood why everyone kept warning us to stay away from the Mau Maus. After all, these guys were my family. They would die for me, and so when I was with them, I was invincible.

Nicky and my other two uncles would always give me a quarter to spend at the local candy store, my motivation for returning time and time again. You would be surprised at how far a quarter would go in those days (average candy price was a penny or two per piece). It didn't matter if Croc was with me or not, either way I was in heaven: sugar induced, cavity creating heaven.

I learned early on in life to appreciate money and the things it could buy. That's why I never passed up on an opportunity to get my hands on money. My mom used to send me and my sisters to a small Pentecostal church on Ralph and Bergin Streets. I loved the atmosphere and was intrigued by the songs the congregation would sing. My favorite hymn was "It's Bubbling, It's Bubbling, It's Bubbling in My Soul." That was a real toe tapper, a tune that you would find yourself humming throughout the rest of the day. The change mom gave us to place in the offering tray was my real focus. My contribution always went to the local candy store, not God. Sundays were sweet for all the wrong reasons. These few joyous pleasures were always overshadowed by the reality of my world. Inside the church, looking around, everything seemed perfect, but once you stepped outside, the ugliness was there to greet you, face to face. I was lucky to have my Uncle Nicky and the others as my stepping stones to the truth of what life was really like in the projects. God wasn't going to protect me—my uncles and the rest of the Mau Maus were.

Every now and then I would see the dark side of the Mau Maus, especially if I arrived at their hangout at the wrong time when most of them were getting stoned. Now Nicky was never one to get high. After all, how can you run a business (a gang) while being strung out on heroin? But for my other uncles, they didn't care.

Getting high was just a part of their life—the life of a gangster. I knew it bothered my uncles when I saw them shooting up. I guess they were simply embarrassed, ashamed. Maybe it was the sight of the needles in their arm that caused them to feel guilty, as though watching them get stoned was giving me a bad impression. No worries—I was tough. I could take it. Seeing people slumped over, buzzed was just part of life in the projects. It was everywhere, no matter where you looked.

My Uncle Victor Maldondado, after seeing me enter their hideout, actually yelled at me, "Get out of here, now!" I didn't move; I was puzzled as to why they would want me to leave. When my uncle saw that I wasn't budging, he got up and approached me while shouting in a slur, "You're dead!" I stood my ground, not knowing what to expect. He delivered a closed fisted punch right into the center of my face. There was no pain, just shock. His boney knuckles brutally assaulted my face, causing my nose to stretch awkwardly to one side, almost to the point of breaking. I had been hit in the face before and by guys much larger than me, but I never experienced this kind of brute force, driven with such intense rage. Uncle Victor wanted to teach me a lesson, and I was hardheaded enough to test his limits, just to see how far he would go. I soon learned that he was willing to go all the way!

Even though I was knocked down to the ground, I bounced right back up onto my feet, looked my crazed uncle square in the eyes and said, "Is that all you got?"

Nicky and everyone else watching was disturbed at how severely my uncle hit me. When they saw this cocky eight-year-old punk pop back up onto his feet and face his tormentor, they laughed an awkward sigh of relief. I guess they thought that the drama was over as quickly as it began. Wrong on all counts! There was another lesson to be taught to this tough little eight year old, and the teacher would be my uncle's boiling temper. He chased me out the door and being one with my instincts, I ran as fast and as hard as I could, not even stopping to see if he was closing in on me. It took me almost five blocks to build up enough courage to slow down and look behind me. That was when I realized that I wasn't being chased any more. It was safe for me to stop running now. I still occasionally looked over my shoulder while catching my breath, just to be on the safe side.

As the city bus pulled to a stop, allowing its passengers to enter and exit simultaneously, I quickly entered by the back door exit, trying to be invisible to the authority: the driver. He saw me, but instead of kicking me off, he ignored me. The sight of the blood gushing from my face must have touched him. He cared and showed compassion. He knew I was safe with him, at least for now. Everyone else ignored me. I looked like trouble, and they were right; I was. As my stop approached and I got up to exit through the rear door, I looked forward into the driver's eyes that stared at me through the rearview mirror. His eyes met mine and for a brief moment, we understood each other. Without saying any words, my eyes said, "Thank you," and his eyes replied, "Be careful." I could see the corner of his eyes curl up; he was smiling back at me. I was comforted by his kindness. As I watched the doors close behind me, I turned and headed home. I never gave that bus driver another thought, ever!

This was what life was like being an eight-year-old living in the projects. It was far from perfect, but I didn't know any better. My only goal was to beat down others before they beat me down.

and to grow up to be the mirror image of my idol, Uncle Nicky. I was becoming one with the streets. Years would pass and nothing would change. Lessons were taught by me to others just as others taught me. I was getting bigger, and yes, tougher and wiser too. I was still looking out for my brothers while they looked out for me. That was our way. When help was needed, nothing else mattered.

I was now ten years old, a double-digit age and feeling like I was all grown up. I was still a smaller framed kid, but being tough as nails, it really didn't matter. They (any opposition) knew me and gave me a wide berth. Yes, I still fought and was developing my own internal rage, an anger that I didn't understand. It controlled me. I did consider myself to be a fair-minded person, giving grief only to those who deserved it. This was a lesson I learned from Uncle Nicky, and I was proud of it, of him. If one of the Mau Maus were in trouble, Nicky and my other uncles would put their lives on the line to come to the rescue. I was learning that family was more than sisters and brothers, cousins and aunts. The family of a gang was far deeper, blood deep, bone deep—until death do us part, literally.

One day, while walking home through a nearby park, Croc and I heard some screaming up ahead. It sounded like Cheddar. Croc and I rushed directly into battle. These five dudes were robbing Cheddar (as if he had anything worth stealing). Croc and I started ripping these idiots apart, without letting up for a moment. We were beating these assaulters down. If someone didn't stop us, we would have beaten the life out of each and every one of them—severe punishment for a stupid crime; the code we lived by. A couple of older (brave) girls standing by decided it was time to break up this confrontation. One grabbed Croc while the other one pulled

30   me free. I continued to kick and punch at my prey. Soon all was quiet in the park. We were escorted back to our apartments in the area called 4th Walk. When I reached my place, my grandmother came to the door to see what all the fuss was about. My female escort started to explain what had happened, detailing how Croc and I came to Cheddar's rescue. I stood there listening, with pride and no regrets. Then, my Uncle Victor came barging in. He was the same uncle who delivered that devastating punch to my face a couple of years earlier; the same uncle whose embarrassment of being seen as a heroin user caused his rage to get the better of him and me. This guy still had some serious anger issues.

As my Uncle Victor entered the apartment, he overheard me telling my story to my grandmother, but unfortunately, he only heard the part about me and Croc fighting in the park. He didn't hear or ignored the part about my coming to Cheddar's rescue. His rage kicked in once again, but this time I had nowhere to run. Reaching out with his right arm, he grabbed me by the neck and in one swift motion he picked me up and held me in the air with my feet dangling below me. Walking across the apartment, he continued holding me in his grip. I was completely helpless. Once in the bedroom, he slammed the door behind him, dropping me to the floor at the same time. "So you think you're a gangster, eh?" he yelled while his eyes burned deeply into my soul. I felt like I was staring at the Devil. Reaching behind him, he grabbed the first thing he saw, a broom handle, the one I used for street hockey or stick ball. Whack! His blow was delivered right down on top of my head. My knees buckled, but I stood firm, glaring back into the blackness of his soulless eyes. Seeing me face him like a man, he continued beating me with that wooden handle. Whack, whack,

whack! I felt the dizziness with each strike. His rage was intensified with my determination to face the beast. Here I was, a ten-year-old kid, and he couldn't make me cry. All he could do to me was knock me out and finally, once I was down on the floor and completely unresponsive, he stopped his beating. The lesson was over.

This wasn't the first time he beat me and definitely not the last. For some reason, he didn't like it when I fought back. Maybe he saw something in me that he didn't see within himself. Perhaps I reminded him of the demons that lived inside of him—demons he couldn't beat down. I was an easy target for him to use as an outlet for his rage. His anger was easily set off, and if I was nearby, it was going to be another bad day for me.

One day I decided to venture off by myself and go visit my dad. He had a place over on Livonia and Rockaway in Brownsville. Dad wasn't home. I really wanted to see him, so I decided to hang around and wait, and wait and wait. After three hours, when it started getting dark, I gave up on my plans of spending time with my father and started thinking about my trek back home. I made a series of mistakes that day. I paid dearly for them.

My first error in judgment was leaving without telling anyone where I was going. My mother was frantic and had the entire family looking for me. Even my adopted brothers were involved in the search. My second mistake happened when I saw a police car stopped up ahead, near my dad's place. I was feeling rather tired and saw no reason why I couldn't ask them for a ride home. New York's finest came through when I needed them. It was an interesting ride: the radio was hissing mumbled messages while my two escorts were on constant look out, scanning the scenery in every direction. To everyone on the outside looking in, I must have looked like an important arrest. I felt good! As the squad car approached my home in Kingsborough, I could see the worry on my mother's face; she was still hopelessly searching for me. My third and final mistake for that day was not getting out of the car and running as fast as I could, in any direction.

Seeing me in the back seat of the cruiser as the cops pulled to the curb, my mother told everyone to keep quiet and not say or do anything. "Wait until the police leave," she kept instructing over and over again. They all obeyed as I was handed over to Mom. Once that cruiser turned the corner and was completely out of sight, my mother's brother, crazy Uncle Victor, grabbed me and hauled me off to that back bedroom for another dance with the Devil. My mother did not intervene. "You were a very bad boy," she explained to me later on. In her eyes, I deserved it. I didn't understand how she could allow me to be beat down like that. I never understood it!

On the positive side, his constant beatings hardened me and made me tougher than leather. I could be on the street, in a fight, and never had to worry about how bad someone could hurt me. No one could ever beat me like my uncle did. He would hit me like he was fighting a full grown man, and I would take anything and everything he had to offer. I was developing my own anger issues, a trait I inherited from my crazed Uncle Victor.

Even my grandmother knew he was overzealous when it came to disciplining me. Sitting at the dinner table one night, I asked my grandmother if she could please warm my soup; it had gone cold. Uncle Victor barked at me to sit there and eat it. I argued that I didn't want to eat cold soup. He punched me so hard upside the head that my nose and ear started to bleed. My grandmother, while holding a compress tightly against my head, yelled at him in Spanish, "Usted lo matará un día de éstos!" (You'll kill him one of these days). Crying, she then proceeded to kick him out of her house while continuing to sooth my wounds. He wasn't welcome there anymore. I admired her strength.

Not very long after the soup incident, something strange happened to my family and my world. A radical change was about to touch me and all I held dear to my heart. This event would take me years—no decades—to fully comprehend. It all started when this strange white preacher from Pennsylvania suddenly showed up in the projects. His name was David Wilkerson. His mission was to preach to all of the different gangs in order to show them that there was a better way to live. He wanted to replace their weapons with Bibles and to trade in their anger and distrust for love and acceptance. All I knew was that this insane white guy came to my neighborhood, my streets, my family, and changed everything. Next thing I knew, Uncle Nicky was taken away; I had no idea where to. I waited for his return, visiting the Fort Green projects often, expecting to see Uncle Nicky sitting there; he never was.

I never saw the man I knew and admired again. Nicky was gone, forever. Sure, he eventually came back to the projects, but as a changed man, a different man, and as stranger to me. I mourned the loss of my uncle Nicky. *Why were Nicky and my other two uncles now talking trash about peace and love and compromise and harmony?* I pondered to myself while continuing on my own journey. I would never really understand what they were up to. I didn't know what David Wilkerson's Teen Challenge program was, and I really didn't care. I learned quickly to care only about what was important to me: my own survival. The Mau Maus would have to continue without my uncles, if that was at all possible. There was now a void on my streets and as a ten year old, I was determined to fill the void. Yes, I still had some growing to do and some learning along the way, but I was ready for anything.

Proverbs 23:13

Do not withhold discipline from a child; if you punish him with the rod, he will not die.

Chapter 3: Saved by a Crazy Lady

Death was no stranger to me and my friends. If you heard a siren blasting its way through the streets, chances are it was for someone who was in the wrong place at the wrong time. My first experience with death was food related. There was a guy over in the 3rd Walk who owned a bunch of chickens. When it came time to slaughter them, a crowd of kids would gather and eagerly watch with anticipation. He would grab the chickens one at a time and make quick business of the kill. Seeing the chickens dangling from his grip always reminded me of my many trips to the back bedroom with my uncle. The crowd gathered and settled in for the show; it was time to let the killing spree begin. This guy would grab onto their neck and with one quick twist rip the entire head off. Once he let go of the chicken, he would reach for another while we all watched in amazement as these poor decapitated birds ran around trying to hang on to whatever life they had left in them. The older kids would laugh, but I never understood the humor. It seemed like a waste to me, a waste of life and a waste of food. I knew hunger all too well. There were plenty of days when my breakfast, lunch, and dinner consisted of one thing: mayo sandwiches. Mayonnaise would become a staple in my diet for the rest of my life. I never had any guilt when I was caught stealing food. It was a matter of survival, and I did survive.

It was another of many sad days when we moved to 739 Miller Avenue in Brooklyn. East New York was very much like Kingsborough in some ways and in other ways totally different. I was now living two boroughs away from my brothers and those I cared about. Sure I made friends, but compared to my Kingsborough pals, they were at lot softer, not as tough, and not as loyal, even though they thought they were real roughnecks.

I remember hanging with five of my new acquaintances one afternoon. We were just heading to the store, minding our own business. My mother had bought me a five-speed chopper bicycle (the only bike she ever bought me). I was sitting on it while two of my new friends went into the local pharmacy to pick up some necessities. Out of nowhere, these three large black thugs approached, ordering me to get off of my bike. There was no way I was going to give up my bike to these 18 year olds. A fight started immediately. My three new friends didn't waste any time running for safety, leaving me along to defend myself and my bike. If this was in Kingsborough, my friends would have fought to the death, if needed. There was no such loyalty here.

The fight lasted only three minutes before I was knocked out cold. My remaining two friends saw me on the ground when they came out of the store and immediately started asking what was going on. Why wasn't it obvious to them? I was on ground dazed, confused, and bleeding. Didn't they see three black guys heading down the street with my brand new, two-day old bike? They did help me back home as I was in no condition to walk anywhere by myself. My inner thoughts raced with seeking revenge. This was not going to be the last they saw of me. I also promised myself never to be left vulnerable again. This was when I got my first knife. Simple logic: mess with me and you bleed.

Now I was thirteen years old, and my attitude quickly became the core of my reputation. My mother came to the school so many times to deal with my behavior that the staff used to joke about sending me to my mother's office, the room in which she and I knew all too well. My teachers joked about how I should become a lawyer because of my ability to talk my way out of any situation. Every staff member was overjoyed the day I graduated and headed over to Gershwin Junior High on Lyndon Boulevard. They didn't have to deal with me and my anger issues anymore. Everyone at my new school knew I had been robbed six months earlier. A lot of the boys from my neighborhood went to this school, and so the word spread quickly about how I stood there and fought for my bike, fought until I was knocked out cold.

Being tough enough to stand fast and face adversity wasn't enough. There were always those who thought they were tougher and felt compelled to challenge me. Like me, they couldn't settle being second best. Arriving at a new school, a middle school where there were kids of all ages and sizes, I would be asked to prove myself one more time, and this time the pay off would be huge. There was a gang of Puerto Rican kids known as the Ghetto Brothers. They had two chapters: the regular Ghetto Brothers and the Junior Ghetto Brothers. The leader of the Juniors heard about my fight and how I tried to keep my bike from being stolen. He wanted to test me to see if the rumors were true. The fight began with his hitting me, and at that point, my instincts kicked in. From a spectator's point of view, the battle must have seemed unfair; my foe was a rather large ninth grader and here I was a much smaller seventh grader who must have seemed like an easy kill, but I wasn't. The bout lasted for over 20 minutes, and finally we simply collapsed onto each other, too exhausted to throw another punch. We both bled; there was no winner or loser. I proved the rumors to be true. The two of us became best friends from that point on.

I was now a part of a gang. Unlike hanging with my brothers back in Kingsborough, in contrast, the East New York Junior Ghetto Brothers were organized with structure and long-reaching arms within the community. If anything, we were more like the Mau Maus, and that made me feel strong, powerfully strong. Instead of having to work my way up the ranks like most do, I was given the position of Warlord. My responsibility was to be the liaison between the Junior Ghetto Brothers and other gangs wanting to rumble with us. There was an unwritten code that everybody followed: a set of conduct rules. Before a rumble would start, the Warlords would meet and discuss how the conflict would take place, which weapons would be used, and time and location confirmed.

When the Ghetto Brothers were not fighting, our primary responsibility was getting high and stealing lunch money from anyone in our sights (I liked to think of it as paying their dues). We had many enemies within the neighborhood: The Jolly Stompers, Back Stabbers, and Tomahawks. The Tomahawks were a black gang of older guys from my old stomping grounds. I knew many of them personally and, therefore, I never really had many problems with them. The older Ghetto Brothers gang and the Tomahawks conflicted all of the time. My biggest problem, as a Junior Ghetto Brother, was with the Jolly Stompers. These guys had no class. When they beat you down, they would start stomping on you until you were either knocked out or worse. You can see where they got

their name from. Same applies to the Back Stabbers, not a name I
would be proud of.

Now that I was fourteen years old, I was finally starting to fill out, physically. My body was starting to catch up with my mind. I was armed, dangerous, and yes, I was cool.

The Jolly Stompers and the Junior Ghetto Brothers got into a rumble one day—this would be the day when I shot someone for the first time. It wouldn't be the last. As I entered into battle, I was armed with my two knives, one holstered on each ankle, as well as carrying a loaded zip gun (a single shot weapon made using a metal tube for a barrel and rubber bands for a firing mechanism). I was surrounded by five Jolly Stompers, and they were about to come down on me. I pulled out my zip gun, took aim, and fired right into the middle of them. Immediately, one of the Jolly Stompers screamed out in pain and went down. My .22 caliber projectile found the meaty part of his leg and took him out of action. The other four boys were shocked and froze in their steps, giving me just enough time to break out of there and find safety within my fellow Ghetto Brothers' cluster. The fight continued, and I joined in. Suddenly the cops showed up in force. They entered right into the middle of the chaos and used the only tactic they knew for breaking up a rumble: they started beating us with their night sticks. We tried to scatter, but there were just too many cops. Being predominately Spanish community and being white cops, their objective was to strike out at anyone that wasn't white, including the bystanders who were gathering on the sidewalks to watch the action. It was craziness, sheer chaos. I lost a lot of respect for New York's finest that night; they were now just another rival gang— thugs.

40   Another rumble I recall was against the Back Stabbers. They had cut up one of our boys real badly and as far as the Ghetto Brothers were concerned, there was hell to pay. The rumble was set and the weapons agreed upon. There were 60 Back Stabbers facing off with 50 Ghetto Brothers. We recruited some of the older Ghetto Brothers, just to help even up the balance between the two gangs. During any battle, the gang's president, vice president, and warlord were always put into the middle of the group, protected by their foot soldiers. I was in my place to the left of the vice president, Gabriel (a good friend and a valiant warrior). When Gabriel and I fought like this, we were united as one warrior, four arms and four legs of meanness, ready to take out anyone who broke through our ranks.

Just as both sides were ready to advance onto each other, we heard a commotion coming from the middle of the street. Apparently, a crazy lady entered right into the middle of the battle field and was screaming at the top of her lungs in Spanish. I couldn't see her from where I was standing, but apparently she had gotten the attention of everyone—nobody moved. I could hear her screams mixed in with the hums of confusion coming from everyone else there. Her voice was travelling through the crowd as if she had a purpose, a mission of her own. Then, like the parting sea, the crowd cleared a path; I could finally see this crazy lady's face. I yelled, "Mommy?" Her eyes met mine and before I knew it, she approached me, grabbed my left ear, and almost lifted my entire body off the ground while smacking me across the face and cursing me out in both Spanish and English. That crazy lady was filled with rage as she dragged me off the battlefield. Even as we approached Lyndon Boulevard, she didn't slow down, crossing the busy road, blinded by her anger. Cars screeched to a stop, honking horns, and missing us by inches, if that. Everyone watching did so with a dropped jaw.

While being dragged through busy traffic, I looked back and could see the rumble starting. I tried to break free from my mother's vice-grip hold on my left ear, but she wasn't letting go. The rumble continued on without me. How embarrassing! What is it with my family and my left ear? This is the ear that my mother's brother, Uncle Victor, wacked during the cold soup incident years earlier. Thanks to him I was left with permanent hearing loss on the left side. Now, here I am being dragged by my mother, using the same ear.

Gabriel, who usually stood on my right, was shot and killed during that rumble. At first, I was angry for missing the chance to fight alongside of my fellow Ghetto Brothers. As I approached my friends the next day, I could tell by the look on their faces that something horrible had gone wrong. That was when I first heard about Gabriel. As the words were leaving their mouths, my world started moving in slow motion. My brain was trying to process the details as they were explained to me. The words "Gabriel" and "shot" and "dead" were echoing—everything else audible faded. I was devastated. I cried like a baby, openly cried, and I didn't care who saw me. I was hurt and needed time to heal. The anger within me boiled over. I wanted revenge, and I always got what I wanted.

As the horror settled in and I had no more tears to shed, the reality snapped back into the here and now: I started absorbing the details of Gabriel's last moments. He took a bullet in the left side of his head, a bullet that would have found me as its target if I had stayed for the fight. I pondered why the events happened the way

42 they did. I should have taken the bullet for my friend. That was supposed to be my job.

Ephesians 4:31

Let all bitterness, and wrath, and anger, and clamour, and evil speaking, be put away from you, with all malice.

Chapter 4: The Rat Pack

Every waking moment of each and every day was started with thoughts about Gabriel. The sorrow I experienced was as deep as a knife wound, and it wouldn't heal. My insides ached. I had known hurt before, but it was nothing like this. Being knocked out by an aggressive enemy was nothing compared to the suffering I was enduring at the lost of my friend. My world was now constantly out of focus. My drive and ambitions were gone. I was sucked deep down into this hole and couldn't find a way out of the blackness. If I didn't figure out how to resolve this, I would surely perish. Then, it dawned on me; I saw the answer (actually I heard the answer being whispered to me by my subconscious). It repeated, "Look to the future and prepare for battle." A smile slowly replaced my frown. A plan started to hatch. It was so simple. I realized I would have to put this chapter behind me, and the only way I knew how to do that was by demanding an eye for an eye, a tooth for a tooth, a Back Stabber for a Gabriel. I started living each and every moment prepared for my revenge—always prepared.

Walking down the street a few months after the death of my friend, I couldn't believe my eyes. Up ahead were three Back Stabbers, standing alone. I couldn't believe my luck. It was as if Gabriel was sitting on my shoulder whispering into my good ear, "Go get them." I obeyed. I now knew what it was like to face an enemy without a care for my own safely. My one and only goal was to set an example to all of the other Back Stabbers that you don't mess with the Junior Ghetto Brothers; you don't mess with me. I charged into the conflict with a determination I had never known before: I was a killing machine, armed and ready for action. I had visions of being nothing less than victorious. There was no stopping me.

The streets were getting more and more dangerous, especially for a higher-ranking gang member like me. The two knives strapped to my ankles weren't enough for the kind of protection I needed. My zip gun was awkward and clumsy and not very reliable. I decided to add a .22 caliber pistol to my list of must-have weapons (a full clip with one in the chamber). My blades would serve me well when I was in close hand-to-hand combat. The .22 caliber would give me the advantage when I was at a reasonable distance from my target. I was ready for anything, including my rage-induced revenge.

Once I saw the three Back Stabbers up ahead, everything else in the world went blank. It was just me, my .22, and those murderers. I pulled out my gun and released the safety as I started running full speed towards them. They didn't even see me coming, that is, until I started firing at them. As soon as the first shot fired, the three of them started running towards the nearby stairs leading down to an adjacent borough. With each of my steps, I let a round go. *Pop, pop, pop, pop* could be heard breaking through the silence of the night. I was almost on top of them. I continued to empty my clip. *Pop, pop, pop.* You would think that I would have at least hit a couple of them. Nope, not even one. Not one bullet found its mark! I couldn't believe how lousy my aim was. Out of ammo and still heading towards the three goons, I immediately went into plan B. I quickly reached down and grabbed my two blades. With raised arms, I continued the chase. Everything happened so fast. It must have taken no longer than ten to fifteen seconds from the time I fired my first shot until all three of them were heading down the stairs being chased by me with blades drawn. I wasn't going to let them get away. I continued my chase, rounding the top of the stairway, ready to follow them into the depths of Hell, if needed. As I started down the stairs, two or three at a time, I noticed that it was indeed the Gates of Hell I found. On the bottom landing, I was shocked to see the rest of the Back Stabbers, dozens of them gazing up at me. I came to a complete stop, and I immediately retreated, in the opposite direction.

Nevertheless, the Back Stabbers were already on their way up the stairs after me. Here I was alone, one against at least thirty. I had a feeling it was going to be a very bad night. I ran for my life. When I reached the East New York side of the hood, I started looking for a means for my escape. They were closing in on me, quickly. If I could only make it to the abandoned tenement building up ahead, I could scurry through a broken window, make my way across, and exit on the other side into my territory, my turf. Maybe, if luck (and Gabriel) were with me, my fellow Ghetto Brothers would see me, come to my rescue, and help me finish the job I started. Gabriel may have been with me, but luck surely wasn't.

As I was running towards that abandoned building, I banged my knee on a fire hydrant, causing me to trip and fall. Not the best thing to do when you have an enemy within a few feet of catching up with you. I remember falling to the ground and thinking to myself, "Oh shit!"

The Back Stabbers were on me instantly, without delay, without

46 mercy. I remember feeling the first couple of blows, feet and fists assaulted every inch of my body. The pain was sharp and intense with each and every blow. I tried to fight back, trying to at least take one of them down with me. I never had a chance. I was knocked out cold. It was over. They beat on me until they were convinced I was dead. Even when they assumed I had stopped breathing, the kicks continued, for good measure. Now it was time for them to dispose of the body—my body. I woke up in the exact spot where they dumped me, in the basement of that same abandoned building, the one I was desperately trying to reach.

As my eyes slowly opened, my mind was trying to deal with all sorts of sensations, pain being the main one. My eyes started darting from side to side, trying to make sense of where I was and why I was there. Even my blinking caused every nerve ending in my body to react. When they dumped me in this cold and damp cellar, they covered what they thought to be a lifeless body with cardboard, as though that would keep my remains from being found. I was seriously dazed and confused. Looking to the right and to the left, I was trying to focus. To add to my confusion, I could feel something strange tugging at my feet. *Must be what a broken leg feels like*, I thought to myself as my memory started coming back.

When I pulled the cardboard off of me, I realized that my leg wasn't broken. What I saw surprised me, and yes, confused me as well. I noticed a small dog trying to pull my sneaker off of my bloody foot. What was this pooch doing here, and why did he want my sneaker? It didn't make any sense to me. As I looked around, I realized the severity of my injuries. There was blood everywhere and I was lying right in the middle of it.

I tried to shake my foot free from the dog's grip, but he didn't want to let go. He wanted my shoe, and that was all there was to it. I was in no condition to argue. My eyes started to focus on the dimly lit surroundings, and I was shocked at what I discovered. I screamed in horror as I realized that it wasn't a dog tugging away at me; I jumped up, kicking like crazy. The dog turned out to be the biggest, ugliest sewer rat I had ever seen. His belly was full with my blood, and he wanted more: he wanted meat. He was hungry for my foot. This mammoth rodent wasn't alone. I was totally surrounded by rats, all lapping up my blood. They ate well that night.

I limped outside and slowly made my way home, trying to remain invisible to any lingering Back Stabbers that might still be out there. Eventually, I healed. Nothing was broken—just a lot of cuts and bruises. I still wanted revenge, desperately.

As I turned fifteen years old, I was seeing in myself a man developing. I stood tall and was no longer the smallest within our group. One day some of my fellow Ghetto Brothers and I were just hanging out minding our own business, drinking booze, sniffing some glue, and being cool. All of a sudden cops pulled up. It was like something you see in the movies. S.W.A.T. was on us in seconds. We had no time to react. We were thrown up against a wall. While our legs were kicked out into the spread-eagled position, they shouted, "Spread 'em!"

I was frisked. They discovered my two blades as well as the .32 caliber I had concealed in my waistband. Ever since those Back Stabbers left me for dead, I swore I would never be caught unarmed again. I would always be able to protect myself, and there is no better gun to do the job than a .32 caliber (small, easy to hide, yet it punches with deadly force).

The cops took us to their precinct and called our parents. Strangely, I was never charged with possession or weapons violation. Instead, they allowed the justice of my mother's wrath to deal with me. Less paperwork that way, I guess. They locked me and my mother in a small room. The only furniture in there were a table, two chairs, and a large file cabinet. My mother, after initially smacking me with her hands, used every piece of furniture in that room to hit me. Yes, even the file cabinet took flight, landing on top of me, trapping me on the floor. She then grabbed the cabinet, with a strength I had never seen before, and tossed it out of the way while coming down hard on me with a chair. While that chair had me entangled, the other chair soon followed. I tell you, my mother was tough in those days. Wherever I ran in that room, the furniture followed. The cops allowed this to continue for over 20 minutes before coming to my rescue. Were they trying to save me or their furniture?

Apparently, they told my mother that I was sniffing glue. That is what sent her over the edge. She thought that her son was now a drug addict. When the cops called my mother and told her what I was up to, she came to the police station armed with a baseball bat. Seeing this, the cops took it away from her, thinking they were saving me some serious bodily harm. My mother didn't need the bat; furniture would do just fine. When we finally got home, my mother called my father, telling him that I (his son) was a junkie, a no-good gangster, and a menace to the family. She wanted to kick me out and demanded that my father take me off of her hands, now! She was done with me. My father never came.

Even though my sisters occasionally caused my mother some

grief, I was the real challenge for her. In her mind she would give me one last chance to straighten myself up. The best way to do this was to gather us up once again and move as far as she could from the source of her grief: my friends, the Ghetto Brothers. Our next home was in Linden Plaza. Little did she know that my gang life had not even begun yet, and the Lindon Plaza streets would not tame the beast that lived within me. I was one lucky kid; I had a mother who held in her heart plenty of last chances for me.

Leviticus 19:18

You shall not take vengeance or bear a grudge against the sons of your own people, but you shall love your neighbor as yourself: I am the Lord.

Chapter 5: Do the Hustle

The Linden Plaza apartments were a cluster of eighteen-story buildings, with approximately twenty (two- or three-room) apartments on each floor. This is also where I met the Linden Boys, a group of young men who minded their own business and looked out for one another. Even though they were cons and would hustle whenever the opportunity presented itself, they were nowhere near what we considered to be a gang. If you were a gang and had a hustle going on, you were expected to pay a street tax. Not being affiliated with any organized gang, the Linden Boys were exempt from any and all taxation.

My favorite hustle was a dice game named C-Low. I became really good at throwing the dice. I practiced during every spare moment I had. I could slide the dice just the way I wanted them to land, giving me the advantage every time. There were other gangs nearby, each with their own style of hustle. We had to keep an eye on all of them to protect our own interests. One gang that comes to mind was called the Five Percenters, a group of thugs who first organized themselves within the prison system, only to spew their nastiness out on my streets, the streets of New York.

It was at the Linden Plaza apartments where I met Mickey, my friend and mentor. When Mickey first saw me in action, he was impressed with my cool demeanor and slick, sleight-of-hand techniques with the dice. He started a conversation of mostly small talk before coming right out and asking me if I owned a gun. Not really knowing him and his motivation, I said I didn't while reaching back to confirm that the bump in my waist band was still there, my .32 caliber. The conversation ended. I didn't realize it at the time that Mickey was sizing me up to work alongside of him. The next day he approached me and handed me a package. As I peered inside, I found a nickel-plated .32 caliber pistol with ammo and a custom made holster. I was impressed. He told me to keep myself and the gun as low key as possible. "The gun stays hidden unless you need to protect me or yourself!" he explained firmly.

I understood. I was now working for Mickey. I was now selling drugs. I was now a lifeline between heroin addicts and the psychedelic place they so desperately wanted to be.

At a local bar, known for drug trafficking, I became a familiar face. Here I was, a 15-year-old kid working my hustle at a sleazy bar. I got to know pimps and their girls, pushers, clients, staff and more importantly, the local cops who made it their business to skim our hard-earned cash whenever they could flex enough muscle to get away with it.

One day while I was minding my own business enjoying a game of C-Low, one of the hookers noticed my sleight-of-hand dice throwing technique and decided to take her revenge. I guess she didn't like the fact that I had earned money a lot faster and cleaner than she did. She stood up from the game and headed my way. Her hand stretched out with razor exposed, and she came within inches of slicing my throat. My instincts kicked in and with one clean blow, I knocked her out with my closed fist. I didn't like hitting girls, but what was a guy to do? That "ho" was quick to slash, but I was quicker.

Of course, her pimp got in my face and started threatening me. This was when I felt I had no other options; I pulled out my new nickel-plated side arm and aimed it directly at his face. Mickey was trying to cool things down. He was standing next to the pimp, almost whispering in his ear. I had no idea what he was saying, but whatever it was, it wasn't working. The pimp's brother entered the room and got an eyeful of the tension, with his family stuck right in the middle. He immediately went into protection mode. He approached me with hostile intentions, so I reached behind and pulled out my loyal old .32 caliber friend. I was now standing with both hands armed and dangerous with one gun pointing directly at the pimp's face and the other ready to inflict a deadly chest wound on his brother. Mickey was feverishly working the pimp to get him to stand down. All I knew was that I really wanted to shoot someone; I didn't care who. It was an overpowering sensation, and I was having a hard time controlling it. I could feel my two index fingers tightening against the triggers. I wasn't afraid of my own death; instead, I was embracing it. When you meet someone who has a gun and isn't afraid of dying, you better run as fast and as far as you can.

As quickly as it started, it was as over. The tension was gone. Mickey was helping me lower my arms and telling me that there would be no bloodbath today. The hooker was now up on her feet being severely disciplined by her pimp for starting the whole thing. As fate would have it, that pimp and everyone who worked for him would soon become my good friends. Mickey and I would spend a lot of time doing our deals while the hookers did theirs.

A couple of months later, my anger would once again rage when I heard the news that Mickey was killed. I always wondered by whose bullet did Mickey fall? This was the second time when a close friend fell victim to the streets. I knew he wouldn't be the last. This time I cried in secret, with hidden tears.

Dealing in drugs had its ups and downs. The money was good, but the dangers were immense. Even though I never sold drugs to the general population, I still searched for a better, safer way to earn cash. I soon found it: baseball. If you were good enough, you could get involved in a street game where big money would be on the line. It was a payday bonanza for the winners but a financial pain in the wallet for the losers. The team could make between five hundred to one thousand dollars per game, more by playing a double header. These baseball games were almost as organized as the big leagues but with a lot less money involved. I became a strong player and even had a major league scout check me out a number of times, but nothing would ever come of it; the streets' lure was simply too powerful for me. Nothing else really mattered. Baseball was my hobby, but the darkness of the street was my life.

My mother decided that she needed to do something to help me find the right path to follow into manhood. She was convinced that I was going to die on the streets. She was tired of anticipating that dreaded knock on the door by the cops to inform her that I was a victim of gang violence. Mom was going to make one last effort to save my ass. She literally sold all of her living room furniture so she could afford to send me to the Eastern Military Academy. What a nightmare!

Predominantly attended by richer, white kids, the Eastern Military Academy was a not place where you sent poor, Spanish kids. Seeing me, a poor Spanish kid from the projects, enraged them. The odds were stacked up against me. Three or four times a month I would find myself enduring another beat down. I did get some revenge by occasionally taking a large bat into the bathroom when one of my attackers was sitting in a booth with his pants down around his ankles. Now that was sweet, seeing the look on his face as I kicked opened the booth door and came down hard with my street-style justice. I literally beat the crap out of him; it was fun. The ones who experienced my revenge never did bother me again, but there were so many others. My torment never ended. Even though I got busted for fighting, I never ratted out any of my attackers. It was between me and them. Ratting just wasn't in my character. I was asked to leave the academy.

My mother finally built up enough courage to divorce my father. I was happy for her. I thought that she finally did the right thing, that is, until she started dating this ex-prison guy named Jose who would prove to be the Devil in disguise. He was all nice and charming at first, but once he became her next husband (my stepfather), his evil nature surfaced. He used to taunt me whenever he had a chance. He must have felt threatened by me. I know I was by him. One of his favorite tricks was to put a razor blade in my shower soap. He learned this trick when he was in prison. In the joint, prisoners would split a bar of soap and place a razor blade in between the two pieces before bonding them back together again. The person targeted would be minding his own business, aggressively scrubbing his whole body with his soap and wouldn't realize he was cutting himself until he would see his blood flowing down the drain. His horror would be enhanced by the sight of his blood mixing with the warm running water; everything would be covered in red. Deep slashes would cover his entire body. I learned to check my soap, especially when soaping up down below. When

I told my mother about the razor in my soap, she would accuse me of lying. Needless to say, I did not like my new stepfather, and he apparently had no love lost for me.

When I turned 16, I decided not to deal in heroin anymore. I wanted to get into the pot game. It was an easy business to get started. The best part was the guilt-free distribution network I set up for me and my customers. Everybody smoked weed, and it didn't mess you up like the heavier drugs. I slept better at night.

My typical day started with preparing the day's products. I would make up a variety of packages called tres bags, dime bags, and nickel bags. I would also roll between 40 and 50 joints to sell to those who were on a tight budget. Once the day's supply was assembled and packaged properly, I would load up my school backpack and head off to work (I mean school). The backpack worked great because it was easy to carry, easy to access, and from a distance, I blended in with the other students. The big difference, of course, was that I never carried school books like the rest of the students.

Selling pot at my age was a win-win situation. Adults who got busted for dealing heavier drugs would do some prison time, and if they were repeat offenders, their time behind bars would be substantial. Luckily, I was never busted, although I often got stopped by the cops. They would simply push me up against the wall and force me into the position. Once they grabbed my backpack and confirmed the contents, they would turn and walk away with my stash, allowing me to continue on my way. They knew I had the best pot around and as I said earlier, everybody smoked pot in those days, including cops! I never did let it bother me that a day's worth of income was gone—I preferred to simply refer to it as street tax. We all have to pay our dues.

I did get arrested for other offences but being underaged, all they could really do to me was give me a beating and call my mother. In those days there was no such thing as child abuse or children's rights. You either learned to take it or you were lost, beat down, and broken forever.

During my seventeenth year, trouble and I were continuing our dangerous dance. I was once again in trouble with the law and facing charges which could have easily landed me into a juvenile detention facility, but lucky for me, I had recently enlisted in the army. By the time my court date arrived, I was only two weeks away from deployment. The judge glared down at me from high atop his perch and scowled, "Against my better judgment I am going to let you walk away from this one. Go serve your country and do something constructive with your life. Don't ever let me see you in here again. Now get out of my sight!"

I obeyed and within 12 days, I was off to Fort Bragg. The army life was tough, but I was tougher. I sailed through boot camp, but because of my flat feet, I was not assigned to a permanent post. My military career was short and sweet. From that day forward, I would be considered a veteran with an honorable release and that made me proud. God bless America!

After my discharge, I was back home without a home. I needed a place to stay. My mother didn't want me, even though I was sending her most of my military pay checks. I kept between 25 and $30 to hold me over for the month until my next check; everything else went to my mother. My needs were few. I had free clothing and free room and board. A few dollars here and there for smokes and beer was all I required.

Once I was back in the projects, I ended up moving in with my aunt in Kingsborough. This would be a short term arrangement until I found an apartment of my own. My stay with her was cut even shorter the day I brought home a girl who ended up staying the night. When my aunt woke up and found me and my guest all tucked in, nice and cozy, she hit the roof. Her ranting was loud enough to wake everyone up in the entire building. Her solution was to kick me out onto the streets, the streets I once called home. I was now a homeless vet with few options.

Even though my experience with the military was for a short period of time, everything on my streets seemed to have changed. My old stomping ground was now foreign to me. My abusive Uncle Victor had completed the Teen Challenge program and was now living in Ohio, starting a youth program of his own called Youth on the Move. Even Croc was gone—arrested and serving time in prison. I ended up hanging out more and more with Cheddar, my other adopted brother from way back when. We became very close real tight friends, just like Croc and I used to be.

Ephesians 6:11

Put on the whole armor of God, that you may be able to stand against the schemes of the Devil.

Chapter 6: I Didn't Do It

Cheddar and I were skilled hustlers and within a short period of time. Our pockets were over flowing with cash. We were generous with our windfall, to a fault. The main benefit was all the girls who constantly swarmed us. They were everywhere. The ladies knew we were cool and just wanted to hang out with us. We obliged. I even started working in a store on the corner of St. Marks and Buffalo. The store owner knew my family and thought he would be helping me out by offering me some sort of job. The duties were mindless, and the salary was chump change in comparison to my other sources of income.

For me, the best part was how my working a full-time job appeared to the authorities; they were watching my every step. Seeing me working regular hours and earning a paycheck must have made them feel a little more at ease. My goal was to get as far beneath their radar as I could. The cops were never really completely fooled. I had my hands in too many things; every time something was being investigated, there was my name, popping up like a beacon. But they were going to have to catch me breaking the law firsthand before they could do anything about it. Even though I was one way or another involved in these criminal activities, I remained detached as much as possible. I always considered myself to be one step ahead of the law and twice as smart. I was cocky!

During working hours, I would get visits from the boys in

Kingsborough's 1st through 7th Walks. Typically there were hostilities between the groups from different Walks. Everyone thought their turf was superior to other territories. While visiting me at the store, everyone behaved. Those were my rules and everyone obeyed. My workplace was like a neutral territory, giving all the opportunity to get to know one another. The tension between the various Walks soon gave way to brotherhood. There was a common ground after all, where anger gave way to socialization. We were becoming tight—one for all and all for one. I think the fact that we were all getting older and wiser had a lot to do with it. Everyone realized that there were more important things to focus on such as girls and money. The more we all stuck together, the more of both we would all get to enjoy. There were still challenges. Now that I was 18 years old, I could no longer rely on a juvenile status to keep me from doing serious time for my activities. As far as the law was concerned, I was an adult with criminal intent.

A bunch of us planned a trip into Manhattan to celebrate my brother Skull's birthday. Twelve of us, including Croc who was recently released from jail, hopped onto the train heading over to 42nd Street to catch a movie. We were all having the time of our lives, smoking weed and sipping down some drinks. Everything was going as planned and everyone was being cool. Then, without warning, Chucky, who was one of the guys with us, and Skull started fighting with two guys from a Manhattan gang; they just popped out of nowhere. As quickly as they appeared, they disappeared.

"What was that all about?" I asked.

"Just some punks' getting smart with us" was the only reply I received.

That's cool, I thought. Then it was back to partying with my boys.

As we rounded a corner, only a few blocks away from the movie theater, we saw the same two punks heading our way, with an army behind them. They were all from the same Manhattan gang. There were only twelve of us, which meant that the fighting odds would be approximately five or six to one, in their favor. My whole life was a constant fight against the odds. Why should today be any different? Let the rumble begin!

The fight was crazy. We picked up anything and everything we could find to help us balance the odds. It felt as if we were fighting every gang member in Manhattan. Croc was surrounded and took a knock down hit to the head with a cane. He was being swarmed. I ran over and jumped onto the group as they continued to beat on Croc. Somehow Croc was able to struggle to his feet. He and I fought back-to-back. We were beating the odds.

Innocent bystanders who had the misfortune to stumble upon our battle were shocked and immediately scattered in every direction, screaming and crying as they fled. Some would accidently get a little too close to the rumble and take a few hits themselves.

For a warrior in battle, it is hard to tell the difference between the enemy and some guy heading home after a long day in the office. It's not like you have time to stop and look them over before beating on them or allowing them to pass unscathed. The rules are simple: if you don't know who to hit, then you better hit everyone, women and children excluded.

The cops were of no help. Even though they were everywhere, the battle raged on. Finally it was time to make our way back to our own turf. These dudes were protecting their territory, and I could respect that. I would do the same if the tables were reversed.

Making our way to the rail station, while continuing to fight, we saw an opportunity to board a soon-to-depart train. As we all jumped on board, the cops singled me and two others out from everyone else. They grabbed hold of me and were able to pull me off the train just as the doors were closing. The train, my escape, with most of my friends, was starting to roll down the tracks without me. Apparently some people were robbed during all of the confusion and for some reason I stood out. It was me and two other guys from Kingsborough that would have to stay in Manhattan and take the rap.

Now any reasonable person would ask, "How on earth did you rob someone while in the middle of a chaotic street fight like that?" The answer is a simple one. I didn't rob anyone. Believe me, I didn't do it. I wasn't there to target someone for a robbery; rather, we had gathered to celebrate the birthday of a friend, my brother Skull. Unfortunately, the other two guys who were busted with me didn't think the way I did. They were there to take advantage of a situation. They were the robbers. We ended up being transported to Riker's Island, one of the dirtiest jails you could ever imagine. For my own protection, I started hanging out with a Puerto Rican gang who called themselves La Familia (the family). While I was in jail, they would be my family. For now, I was safe.

Riker's Island reminded me of Alcatraz, off of the San Francisco coast, completely surrounded by water with nowhere to escape. Most of the inmates on Riker's Island were waiting for their trial date. Few were there to stay for the duration. There had been cases when an inmate would have to endure the rat infestations for up to two years before either being sent off to some larger prison or cracking under the pressure of the filth and subhuman living conditions. When a guy finally breaks, he will do or say anything to cop a plea bargain in order to get off of Riker's. Guilt or innocence doesn't really play a part in this game. The truth will not set you free. The only voice that counts is that of the district attorney. If you have a criminal record, your best option is to keep your mouth shut and listen to what the D.A.'s office has to offer. Sometimes, although rarely, you actually can come out ahead.

The assistant D.A. came to visit me while I was in the Riker's Island holding cell. I was escorted to a small room where I was able to sit face-to-face with my accuser. He started by saying, "If you cooperate with my office, you can walk right now."

I laughed. The plain and simple facts: these two guys who robbed some innocent bystander during the rumble were idiots, plain and simple. But they were from Kingsborough and that carried a lot of weight in my books. As I said earlier, ratting was not in my character. In those days, we believed in loyalty. Unlike those so called want-a-be gangsters who start singing to save their own ass, my lips were sealed. If I wanted you dead, I would deal with you face-to-face, not shoot up your house from the safety of my car, risking injuring your grandmother, or even worse, your children. These were days of honor, and I for one lived by that creed.

My day in court finally arrived, and to be honest with you, I didn't care what happened to me, as long as I didn't have to go back to that hellhole of a jail Riker's Island. As I stood there looking up at the judge, his words echoed throughout the room. He uttered, "It is the decision of this court that you be held in custody for a period of between one-and-a-half years to four years." With that he slammed down his gavel, sealing my fate, for not being a snitch. I swore to myself that this would be the first and last time I go to prison for a crime I didn't commit. I was pissed until I realized that, yes, I didn't do this crime, but how many crimes did I actually commit and get away with? I was now more at peace with my situation.

I was sent to a soft camp in upstate New York named the Mid-Orange Correctional Institute. This would be my permanent address for some time, so I decided to fill my days with as much activity as I could in order to make the time pass easy and fast. Because of my baseball background and after watching my try-outs, the staff was more than happy to accept me on its institutional team. They only allowed the best to play, and I was one of the best they had. The Mid-Orange staff, as in all state prisons, would bet money on their own teams, and so my guards were extremely pleased with me and my performance, especially when they walked away from each game with a little extra spending money in their pockets.

It seems that every time I tried to stay out of trouble, trouble still had a way of finding me. I was in what seemed like a country club prison. I had three square meals a day, I was living in the country enjoying the fresh air, and I was playing my favorite sport daily. I even got my G.E.D. which made me feel extremely proud. I was living the high life and by doing so, like a fool, I let my guard down.

A new inmate—a fat, ugly black dude who had a huge chip on his shoulder—saw me as being soft, an easy target. Just because I walked around smiling at people didn't mean I was soft. What an idiot! One night this moron came up to my cube and demanded that I give him my sneakers and all of my food. One of the first things I did when I arrived there was to place a combination lock inside of a sock, and I stashed it with my other possessions. When I was instructed to hand over my sneakers and food, I didn't say a word. I just smiled, reached for that sock, and smacked him. *Whack!* One hit and he was down for the count. That was all it took to defeat this Goliath. That one shot protected me, but I had to make sure everyone else watching got the message, loud and clear. I continued beating him on his arms and legs. The damage was severe. He would rue the day he messed with this white, Spanish kid. He and his scars will remember me forever.

The guards overreacted. They told me that I should have stopped after he was knocked out. They didn't understand the concept of my sending a message to the entire population saying "if you mess with me, you risk what I might do to you, and yes, I might even kill you." The guards had no other option; their hands were tied. They were going to lose their star ball player. I was going to lose my place at the Mid-Orange "resort."

My new home would be a toilet of a prison called Elmira, easily one of the worse prisons in New York State. I knew about this place. I heard the stories from my uncle who was lucky enough to grace these cell blocks years before. I was surprised that I wasn't thrown into the hole upon arrival. This was the usual method of dealing with violent inmates who needed to learn a lesson in following the prison system's social rules. I later found out that someone had informed the authorities of exactly what happened with the stupid black guy at Mid-Orange. Because of my ball playing skills and being a model prisoner, I was never charged or disciplined. I was just transferred. It was easier this way.

Elmira was a horrible place; it had the stench of Riker's Island, only much worse. Lucky for me, La Familia was there in full force.

66 Since I was already a member from my short stay at Riker's Island, I was a member for life. This gang had spread out to over eighty-five percent of the New York Prison system. I would be okay with them. We all looked out for each other. They were more of a family than a gang. We existed by the same basic rules that I lived by on the streets of Kingsborough. If you messed with one, everyone else would come after you. Once they caught you, it wasn't pretty. I worked out every day and, of course, I played on the institutional softball team.

Elmira was like a world of its own—nothing like I had ever seen before. Older inmates would talk to you if they thought you had potential, a certain spark in your eye. They could tell if you had a talent in areas such as pimping, robberies, or even basic hustling. They would listen to what you knew, then would add their words of wisdom. They were the teachers you would never want your kids to have. They were the professors of institutional physics and street smarts. Once again, I proved to be an "A" student. Time passed. It took one year, ten months, and seventeen days for the parole board to finally open my cage. As I walked outside towards my freedom, I slowly glanced over my shoulder, giving the stench of confinement one last whiff. I mumbled so nobody could hear, "I didn't do it."

Now 20 years old and a free man, there was only one thing I needed to do. I went to my mother's house to get my belongings. I found one bag of clothes she held for me in a closet under the stairs. They stunk of mold and mildew. I asked her where the rest of my clothes were. She told me that the one bag was all there was. Great, I just got out of prison and have no clothes and no money except for the $50 I received upon my release. My mother was looking at me as if I were a stranger. I guess I was. All she wanted to know was when I was going to get out of her sight. I left right away, without saying goodbye or closing the door behind me.

Naturally, I went out to do what I do best—hustle. I took my $50 and went directly to Kingsborough. I was pleased to see my brother Cheddar. He was a sight for sore eyes. I tried explaining my situation to him, but he just kept laughing at me. "What's so funny?" I finally asked. He pointed at me, giggling. I still had on the prison suit they gave me when I got out of jail. I must have been a sight. He put five hundred bucks in my pockets and took me shopping for some new clothes. I ended up staying with him and his family in the building I grew up in. As always, we began to do our hustling, and I eventually paid him back for his kindness. I could always count on my adopted brothers.

I eventually found an apartment in East New York, in the basement of a small, run-down, brick building. My mother lived about one and a half miles up the street from me. I would visit her occasionally, but only when I felt that I had to. She was still living with that demented guy Jose. I really wanted to hurt him. If there was someone out there who deserved to be shot, it was Jose. Maybe one day, but for now I had to pick up the pieces of my life and start putting them back together, one at a time.

I wasn't very long after my release from prison that I got shot for the first time. I was minding my own business, playing some C-Low with some of the guys on the corner of Pennsylvania and New Lots Avenues. Some gang members I didn't recognize decided to help themselves to our hard-earned cash. They actually tried to rob us. When will these punks ever learn? Don't mess with me, my friends, and especially with my money. It was on. Like every other event on the streets, it all happened so quickly. We barely started fighting when the cops showed up from nowhere. Once again, my instincts kicked into autopilot, and I was off running for my freedom. As I ran down the street, dodging here and jumping there, this rather overweight white cop was in chase. There was no way he was going to keep up with me, so he did the next best thing. He drew his side arm and squeezed off a couple of rounds, one finding the fleshy part of my right calf. I went down, rolling on the ground as bystanders watched in horror. That moron was firing his weapon at me when there were innocent bystanders all around me. They started screaming in terror and scattering in all directions. In the confusion, I jumped up onto my feet and hobbled to safety, under the cover of innocent onlookers running for their lives.

I, with the help of friends, made my way to my Aunt Ada's place. She was a nurse and her oldest son, Big Pete, knew a lot about gunshot wounds. If I tried to get help at any one of the hospitals in the area, the cops would have been notified and that would have been the end of it for me. Aunt Ada was my only hope.

Big Pete had all kinds of surgical instruments and was able to help me with my situation. He gave me a full bottle of alcohol and told me to drink it all. I did, and soon the pain started to subside. Then, without warning, I was pinned down and held securely while a long pair of forceps was used to probe the wound, looking for the lead that was tightly lodged within my muscle. That was when the real pain started. As the instrument touched the outer edges of my wound, electrical shock waves of pain and torment overtook my entire body. Slowly the forceps dug deeper and deeper into the bloody hole in my leg. Once it could penetrate no deeper, the tips were opened while it probed for the bullet. I screamed as I fought to free myself from their tight hold on me. Finally, I passed out from the pain. My recovery was quick, although I did have to deal with a slight infection. Most importantly, I now knew what it was like to be on the receiving end of a .32 caliber. I had a greater respect for the pain I would inflict on others. I felt empowered and reluctant, all at the same time. I would need to be more careful, more professional, and more mature. Soon I was back to normal, back to my world of sex, drugs, and rock and roll. I was back on my game, in full force.

Ezra 7:26

Whoever will not obey the law of your God and the law of the king, let judgment be strictly executed on him, whether for death or for banishment or for confiscation of his goods or for imprisonment.

Chapter 7: The Claymont Era

I guess you could say that I should have picked a better class of friends. My true friends were the brothers I grew up with, those who would be willing to die for me. The truth is, the guys I worked with, unlike my friends, were the ones who were most likely to stab me in the back (no pun intended). These were hard core warrior dudes, mercenaries who offered faithful service to the highest bidder. A guy named Kingston, from one of the Caribbean islands, was part of my team, my crew. When it was time to pull off a job, he was always the first one to rush into the task with an eerie eagerness. It was scary.

On one occasion, we were hanging out at one of the local make-out spots, secluded and protected under the cover of night. We would wait until we saw a car parked, with its lights off. We would approach it, keeping the element of surprise as our primary weapon. This mad dog, my partner in crime, would stand at the passenger window while I secured the driver's side.

On one occasion, the driver was terrified to see us—me brandishing a sawed-off shotgun and Kingston armed with a 30/30. Ignoring our commands, he immediately tried to start the car, as if he would have a chance of getting away. I could tell that my associate wanted kill both the driver and his girlfriend. I yelled, "No. Wait a second."

"But they saw our faces," Kingston barked back while itching to squeeze the trigger.

I snapped back without pause, "So what. Who cares? They don't know us. Now point that gun somewhere else."

Kingston obeyed. I placed my shotgun against the driver's face, telling him to sit back; he complied with a look of sheer terror in his eyes. I'll never forget that blank death stare. The next thing I did was tell him to get out of the car, and he did as he was told. We went about our business. Within minutes we were done and nobody got hurt. I saved that driver's life that day, and he knew it.

I was glad when my partnership with Kingston ended. Apparently he had his own goals, which included doing robberies on his own. That way he wouldn't have to share the booty. One day he broke into an apartment and discovered an elderly couple still at home. He beat the wife and murdered the husband in cold blood. I swear ice ran through this man's veins. This wasn't the first life he snuffed, and it wouldn't be the last if he weren't taken down, somehow. The day they busted him, our community cheered as they hauled him off to jail. It didn't take the authorities very long to follow the trail of evidence left behind at the scene of the crime. Once the jury heard from both sides, they came to a unanimous decision. The trial was quick and sweet. Kingston was sentenced to life without the possibility of parole. I breathed easier.

Flatbush was a neighboring borough and there was a ton of money to be made there. If someone in Flatbush wanted to score some weed, we were the dealers they looked for. We owned the Flatbush marijuana business. It was easy money. The cops never bothered us because we stuck with pot and maybe some pills here and there. As long as we paid our dues to the cops, we were pretty much left alone. Those who dealt in the heavy drugs were the main

focus of the narcotics' squad. Nobody respected those who pushed
poison.

We had a supply chain that worked like a well-oiled machine. It started from a gang that we referred to as the Drug Store. Because we dealt only in a volume business, we were given the best product available at the best price. The supply was not without its limits. When the Drug Store was closed, for whatever reason, we had a plan "B" and plan "C," "D," and "E" in place. A guy named Skinny John was our plan "B" and was always eager to make us a deal—to offer us his volume discount. It was a competitive business. Skinny John ended up killing a parole officer, giving him a one-way ticket to the slammer. Gone forever! So much for plan "B."

Claymont was the head of the Flatbush crew. This was one nasty, mean, dirty, fighting dude. He owned a small building on Norstrand Avenue, our headquarters. Claymont lived on the first floor, and we pretty much took over the rest of the building.

We decided to diversify our product line. We were now a one-stop shop for pot, pills, and anything else that would give you a mild buzz. Oh yeah, we also carried a full line of weapons, ammo, and accessories. If we busted into a gun store, we would take every single piece of inventory we could get our hands on and bring it back to Claymont's. You would be surprised at how many guns you could sell, on the same streets, to the same people, time after time. That's what happens when you use a gun and throw it into the river afterwards. Repeat business was good.

An associate of mine named Diamonds worked at a nearby retail store. We decided it was time to help ourselves to the goods, and with Diamonds' insider intelligence, it was going to be an easy take. Of course, Diamonds wouldn't actually take part in the robbery. We decided to use him as our getaway driver. We didn't want him to lose his job, assuming his being in the car would keep his identity hidden from those who employed him.

As we were heading towards the job site, I was in the back seat loading up my new companion, a slick and dangerous 30/30. I, along with my taste in weapons, was evolving. Next to me was my friend Popeye. Diamonds was up front in the passenger seat, and Claymont was driving. As I was loading my piece, I pulled back the breech to put a bullet into the chamber. My hands must have been oily because the breech slipped from my hands slamming it home. *Pa-boom* echoed throughout the car; the interior quickly filled with smoke—dense, stinking smoke. The round barely missed Popeye's left foot. The concussion from the blast still hurt his foot making him react as if he were actually shot. Panic started taking over.

Claymont, Diamonds, and I were faced with a dilemma. If Popeye were shot, and we took him to a hospital, the staff would start asking all kinds of questions. The cops would have been called. Would Popeye follow my example and keep his mouth shut about the rest of us and our activities or would he spill his guts, singing a song of pointing fingers and truthful accusations? Claymont turned the car around and headed back towards home base. We would assess Popeye's injuries along the way. Either way, we would have to abort the mission. We were relieved to see that he wasn't actually shot. No holes. No blood. His injuries would heal.

Later on, Claymont came up to me and said, "Do you realize that if Popeye was actually shot, we would have to bury him in a field ourselves?"

I replied, "I know. I know."

As the words spewed out of my mouth, a sudden feeling of dread started to overtake me. My spark was extinguished. That was the moment that I realized how close I came to having to commit the ultimate sin—killing my friend. Something inside of me changed forever. I always knew I had a soft heart. That day it got even softer.

One of our main money makers was to rob other drug dealers. What are they going to do, call the cops? I don't think so. Claymont wanted to rob his sister-in-law's boyfriend because he was a dealer and was an easy target (he made the mistake of trusting us). I told Claymont that I was not interested. I didn't believe in targeting family. That's just not smart business. I thought that was the end of it until a short time later I heard Claymont's sister-in-law was shot point blank in the head, leaving her to spend the rest of her life severely mentally challenged. Her boyfriend was now on the run from us. He was lucky enough to avoid our wrath and was looking to cop a plea with the D.A.'s office. Ratting was his only survival option. It made the entire crew nervous. He knew too much about all of us. The crew continued looking for him to persuade him to keep his mouth shut. Actually, they were going to simply shut it for him. Unfortunately, he sung like a canary leading to multiple arrests with charges ranging from attempted murder to robbery and weapons' violations. Three of my crew met with some serious prison time, hard time.

Hanging out at Claymont's place was a dangerous occupation, especially if you sat out front on the stoop, as we did daily. If someone wanted to hit us, this was their best opportunity to do some damage within our ranks.

One day we were doing just that, sitting there on the front stoop, smoking a few joints, and planning our next activity. Suddenly out of nowhere a car came barreling around the corner, screeching to a stop a few yards in front of us. It was full of those Caribbean thugs, and we were in their crosshairs. Shots were being fired in our direction. Everybody in that car was armed and taking aim. We dove in every direction you could imagine. Lucky for us, everyone in that car was gifted with lousy aim. We never kept our guns on us. It was too easy to get busted that way. We did have hiding places very close by, and so as each and every one of us dove, we were individually diving towards our own hiding spot, bouncing up instantly, returning fire. When these want-a-be assassins ran out of ammo, they peeled out of there as quickly as they appeared. As they made their way up the street, my crew was popping up from everywhere returning fire. The car took a lot of hits including two from me and my sawed-off shotgun. That was all I could do, one from each barrel.

I use to think that Claymont had a big organization, that is, until I met another dealer who was playing the same game as Claymont but on a much larger scale. This dude owned multiple buildings (Claymont owned one). Drug money goes a long way in the real estate business. He wanted me to take over one of his buildings to oversee the day-to-day operation. It was a lucrative offer. First thing he did was to get me started with a little inventory. He fronted me a few pounds of pot and gave me a building to manage. For security purposes, I decided to take one and a half pounds over to Claymont's place. I couldn't think of a safer place to keep my stash. A day or so later, while over at Claymont's partying with the crew on a half gallon of rum, Claymont decided to make a pass a my new girlfriend Regina.

Regina and I started dating when I was twenty-three years old. We were introduced to each other by Cheddar, and the very first time I saw her, I told her that I wanted to kiss her. I knew she was special. Taking her by the hands, I led her out into the hallway where her passion meshed with mine. It was the most sensual kiss I had ever experienced. I knew then that she was the one.

When I brought Regina over to Claymont's to enjoy the cocktail party ritual, Claymont took it upon himself to cop a feel when I wasn't looking. The moment his hands touched her butt, he spat upon our friendship; he flaunted his disrespect right in front of my face. When Regina told me what happened, I had no other option: I confronted Claymont. I didn't care about who he was or how high up he was on our leadership ladder. Nobody messes around with Regina except for me, period! He wasn't pleased with me and my attitude; nor was I with his. Since I was considered "Psycho Bob" by those who knew me, Claymont knew he would lose this confrontation. He backed down, yet never offered an apology. I was pissed and hurt. "Regina, get your coat. We're out of here," I commanded. It took me a few minutes to say my goodbyes and gather up my belongings. I had one last thing to gather up on the way out.

Something deep inside was telling me to grab the pot I had stashed there. I always listened to that little voice. When I went to my hiding place, all I found was empty space. Now my anger turned to rage. I screamed at everyone there, accusing each and every one of them. The party was over. Claymont was helpful in organizing the search in an orderly fashion. He made an announcement, telling everyone that they had to leave. When they made their way to the door, they were searched (I mean hands against the wall, spread-legged searched). If someone didn't want to be frisked, well, they were frisked anyway. Claymont took half of the folks while I searched the others. Not a single bud could be found. I was now responsible for the lost weed; it would have to come out of my pocket. There would be no profits this week. I was baffled. Who would take my weed? These people were like my family. Something wasn't right.

A week or two later, someone in my crew informed me that Claymont was now selling weed on the streets. This was a task that he always left to others. When I went to check this out for myself, I found Claymont and my weed, together. Realizing that he was the only person who didn't get searched, I confronted him and all he did was deny, deny, deny. I now knew that he didn't care about me or what we had together. All he wanted was to take what was mine. If he couldn't have my girl, then he would take my weed. I wasn't going to get anywhere with this confrontation, so I did the next best thing. I found someone who was dear to his heart and broke him up pretty badly. I no longer considered Claymont or any of his relatives as family. They were strangers to me now. My heart ached for the loss. Claymont soon heard about my actions, even though I kept my identity hidden by wearing a mask when I delivered the beating. I denied doing this terrible thing just like he denied stealing my pot. It was a stalemate. But we both knew.

I had a robbery scheduled, organized by Claymont. A friend of mine informed me that Claymont had given the order that I should be considered collateral damage. He wanted me killed while doing a job so he wouldn't be blamed for my death. Claymont knew that if he openly hurt me, Cheddar and my other Kingsborough brothers would seek revenge like he had never seen before. There would literally be hell to pay. I knew who was supposed to pull the trigger during the robbery, so my plan was very simple: I never turned my back on him during the entire job. He was always in my sights; if he came anywhere close to pointing his gun at me, I would have done him before he knew what hit him.

I could have hit Claymont myself (indirectly, of course), but the consequences would have been devastating. His family would have come after people I love, including Regina. My actions had to be planned out carefully. Claymont and I had some profitable times working as a team. He knew when I was sent on a job, nobody would be killed. I got the job done. I had common sense and reason. Sure, rarely I would have to hit upside someone's head when they weren't paying attention, but for the most part, I was the foundation that my crew could rely on. What a waste to lose all of that over a pound and a half of grass. What a waste.

Leviticus 19:11

You shall not steal; you shall not deal falsely; you shall not lie to one another.

Chapter 8: Down and Out in Ohio

It wasn't very long after the birth of my first son, Louis Saviour-faire, Junior, when my neighborhood started to get a little too hot for me. I was at Regina's house enjoying a day of relaxation when a call came in for me. It was someone from my crew telling me that I should not come back to the apartment. The cops were there in force, asking about me. They were like cockroaches: crawling, searching everywhere, looking for me. I had so much going on the past few weeks, I honestly forgot about my weekly visits with my parole officer. Missing one appointment was not such a big deal, but since I had missed a couple in a row, there was an all-points bulletin issued for my butt. I looked at Regina and said, "Well, I was planning on a trip to Ohio to visit my Uncle Victor. Care to join me?" She eagerly agreed, and with that, my family was westward bound.

You would think that after being abused by my Uncle Victor for so many years the last thing I would want to do was to go and visit him. Truth is, he was there for me, always. When I was in prison, my uncle was the one who would visit me, check up on how I was doing, and like clockwork, he would deposit money into my commissary, just to be sure I had what I needed to get by on the inside. That just proved to me that no matter how strict he was, it was his concern for me that drove him to beat the crime right out of me (or at least try to do so). What touched me most was how he stocked up my mother's fridge every time he was in town. My uncle and I drew closer. He completed me. The scars of my youth were finally fading. Even though he would speak to me about God every chance he could, his words were foreign to me. I was too stubborn (or hardheaded) to actually hear the words he was trying to teach me. My uncle was saved, but I, at twenty-five years old, was still lost in a pit of corruption and sin.

After a few days of showing Regina around Ohio just to see if it was the type of place she could imagine raising our family, I heard on the news about the raid on Claymont's house back in Flatbush. They were still looking for me, and now I made the national news. It was kind of funny at the time, but in retrospect, I should have realized that I did screw up and still had a commitment with my parole officer. Apparently, I was also a person of interest in a number of crimes that were being investigated back home. My debt for skipping parole would soon be paid, in full, all the way from Ohio. But for now I was focused on what was really important to me. It wasn't the drugs or the lifestyle of a gangster that motivated me. Instead, it was the ten perfect little fingers and ten cute little toes of my son. Louis Junior was my everything, my pride and joy, my legacy. What was going on back home really didn't mean anything to me. I didn't give it a second thought although I should have.

Mom and her idiot husband Jose had recently moved to Ohio where the pace was slower and more relaxing. Regina and I finally left Uncle Victor's so Mom could spend a few weeks getting to know her new grandson. At first everything was great. Family bonding can be a beautiful thing, that is, until you start feeling homesick, and Regina was downright ill with missing Brooklyn

I knew what was waiting for me back there, so I was reluctant to leave the calm of Ohio for the chaos of the projects.

Regina and I started to argue more and more until she just couldn't take it anymore. Something had to give. Before she snapped completely, she took my son and left. The pain I felt was more severe than any knife wound. I was hurting, deeply. My aching heart was blinding my judgment. I felt as if I were going crazy, and in some ways, I was. I would call Regina screaming angrily, "Bring back my son!" She ignored me. I would threaten her, "If you don't show up here with my son, there will be dire consequences for you and your family!" Needless to say, she never did return with Junior. Regina knew I had anger issues. She also knew what was best for all of us. That was her gift.

Over the next few weeks, we continued to speak over the phone on a daily basis. I was calming down, yet my stomach still churned deep inside. During our talks, I would tell her how nice Ohio was, trying to convince her to sway from her better judgment; she never did. Her reply was always the same, "You're not seeing me or your son until you resolve your anger issues!" As I said, she was the smart one in the family.

I was running out of options. My last attempt would be to work her sensitive side. The next time we spoke on the phone, I began to reminisce about the day Junior was born. I reminded her of how I remembered the day my son was born when I was at Claymont's house hanging with the guys. Hazel (Regina's mom) called me, shouting something about my becoming a father real soon. I dropped everything, including the full bottle of beer I was drinking, and rushed to be by her side at the hospital. The boys tagged along for moral support. Regina was listening carefully. I continued talking about how drunk I was when I arrived at the ward but sobered up quickly when I was told that my son was delivered a few moments earlier. Regina was adding to my recollection, adding her own memories of that magical day. I continued speaking about how cute my son was, the cutest baby I had ever seen. Regina was laughing along with me, agreeing with every word. "So why not bring him back to me in Ohio?" I asked in a soft and gentle voice. I was convinced now that my soft side was out in the open, she would reconsider her stance. Wrong! The call ended.

I wasn't going to give up that easy. When we spoke on the phone the next day, it was Regina who had the softness added to her voice. She started by asking me if I remembered how small Junior was when he was born. "Did I?" When the doctors said they wanted to keep him in the hospital for an extra week, I started getting really scared. I was afraid that the one good thing I did in my life was about to be taken away from me. That was the longest week, ever.

I suddenly started laughing into the phone and Regina asked what I thought was so funny. I asked her, "Do you remember the chocolate chip story?" I reminded her of the night, not too long after we brought Junior home, when in the middle of a television program, she turned to me and demanded a chocolate chip cookie. I knew that getting Regina her cookie would not be a simple task. I would have to get dressed and holster my 38 before heading outside. Yes, even though I was only going across the street, the Roosevelt Projects were a dangerous place to be, especially at night time. Since I was the guy who sold drugs and guns to these local thugs, it was assumed that I would be carrying a large sum of money. That assumption was usually correct. I continued to recount my memory of the chocolate chip story. At 2:30 in the morning, here I was dashing across the street, trying to avoid bringing attention to myself. I made it back home safely with cookies in hand and was glad when I latched the door behind me. I handed Regina her cookie and after taking one bite, her head tilted back as she fell into a deep sleep. I risked my life for that chocolate chip cookie and there it was, sitting on the table, partially eaten. I was astounded, stunned; I wanted to shoot that cookie. Regina laughed at how I remembered the story. Her memory of that night was a little different from mine.

Regina remembered my going to get her some cookies, but she never thought about how risky going out at night really was. I didn't either. Arming myself was just a natural thing for me, like putting on my shoes. Regina was now talking to me about how dangerous the Roosevelt Projects were. She knew there was a better place to raise a family. Her voice suddenly turned serious, as did mine. We agreed that neither of us wanted to bring up a child the same way we were raised. We wanted the odds to be for our kids, not stacked against them. We didn't want them to experience that deep-rooted panic every time we heard a gunshot echo from somewhere outside of our home. Then, there was a silence over the phone. I could hear Regina breathing on the other side. I was holding my breath. In a soft voice, Regina spoke the words I so desperately wanted to hear. She finally whispered she would bring the baby back to Ohio. She wanted to raise our family in a better environment. My family would soon be complete.

While waiting for Regina and my son to return to Ohio, I was shown around Columbus by various family members, just to see where I wanted to live. There was one section of town on Main

Street that caught my attention. I was informed that this area was part of the ghetto. I laughed thinking to myself that from where I came from this looked like your typical middle class neighborhood. I actually thought that they were pulling my leg about this being a ghetto. Back home, this was the type of neighborhood we targeted for our robberies. We continued our tour to look for that right part of town we could call home.

I started working for a local garbage company in Pataskala, doing 12-hour shifts, 5 days a week. The work was grueling and the pay was substandard, but that was okay by me. I was paying the bills, barely. I sent part of my pay to Regina to help her take care of her daily needs. I also gave a bunch of cash to my mom. I would keep about $20 for myself. I would try to make those few bucks last the entire week, until my next paycheck. Those were lean times.

I had a drinking buddy named Bama, a black man. He and I would get together on weekends and head to a nearby black after-hours club. Even though the cliental was primarily black, all races were welcome, as long as there was no trouble. The bars in town were mostly for white folks, so for a black man wanting to have a drink, it was simpler to go to one of these after-hours clubs where the looks of hatred were nonexistent. Minorities entering a white man's club in Pataskala did so at their own risk. Racism just made Bama laugh. He didn't get it. He was a lover, not a fighter.

One Saturday night, Bama and I were at the after-hours club, enjoying a beer and a game of pool. In walked these three drunk rednecks, each one of them looking for trouble. They were generally ignored. Soon the three turned into nine. As Bama was vying to sink the seven ball into the right corner pocket, he chuckled as he slammed the ball home. One of the rednecks called out, "Hey look, that nigger thinks he can play pool!" Bama ignored him and continued to play. You see, Bama gave them the benefit of the doubt. He thought that because they were drunk, they were allowing the booze to control their actions and words. Bama's heart was big and forgiving.

Seeing Bama ignore their slurs, one of the rednecks took this as a sign of weakness. He walked past Bama, knocking into him intentionally, and then turned around and did it again. Bama decided to speak frankly about what he thought of these intruders and suggested where they should go. The confrontation moved outside.

As soon as everyone was in the parking lot, the guy who started the incident raised his hand as if winding up to deliver a blow. Bama immediately slammed one hit into his face, knocking him out cold. You would think that that would have been the end of it. The other eight morons decided to gang up on Bama, punching and kicking him from all directions. Then all hell broke loose. As they were beating on Bama, not one of them paid any attention to me. Remember, as far as anyone was concerned, I looked very white and being white, they assumed I was not a threat.

I picked up a rather large stick, or maybe it was a branch. As I approached the group, I began swinging. The first two I hit instantly fell to the ground, out cold. This situation was reminding me of the rumbles of my old days in Brooklyn. I was having a lot of fun fighting side-by-side with Bama. Together, we fought off these intruders, knocking them out one-by-one. Eventually, there were five bodies on the ground taking a nap and four others standing there looking at us with a surprised look upon their faces.

Bama and I simply turned and limped away. We were done. Who won the day? I couldn't really say, but I can tell you this, we stuck up for our honor, and it felt really good.

As we headed off the battlefield, we could hear sirens. Both police and ambulances were soon at the sight. Bama and I hid in the trees watching the scene from a distance. The darkness of night protected us from being seen. I was bleeding from everywhere and Bama had a rather large gash in his head. We licked our wounds and slowly we made our way home. I was getting too old for this. I wanted to settle down. I wanted my family back, now.

Finally the day came when Regina and Louis Junior returned to Ohio. Mom, being the perfect Christian mother, decided to kick us out of her place. She didn't want to listen to Regina and me argue all the time and also was not willing to have us sin under her roof. (Regina and I were not married at the time.)

With my savings, I was able to get us into a small hotel on Main Street. It would have to do for now. Being the middle of winter in Pataskala, getting around was a challenge. A car is not a luxury, it is a necessity. There were no trains or busses nearby. I had no way of getting to my job. My stepfather Jose was my only option for a ride to and from work, as long as I paid for the gas. I really didn't like that man. The first couple of weeks travelling with Jose went smoothly, but eventually he became more and more unreliable. He even left me stranded one night, three miles away from home, forcing me to walk in the freezing rain. Why was giving my mom money for food and Jose money for gas? They were living in their own world, so I guess I just wasn't a part of it. I was an alien to them.

When mom kicked me out after Regina arrived, I was never

so happy to slam that door closed behind me. I had enough money for now and as long as it lasted, we would be okay. I would worry about tomorrow, tomorrow. The day finally came when my funds ran out. The hotel management was kicking us out, onto the streets. I called Mom and told her that we were being evicted and forced to live on the snowy streets, in the cold. That must have touched my mother in a special way. Her compassion for my situation was outstanding. She immediately drove over to the hotel and picked us up along with our few worldly possessions. A few miles later, we were pulling up to the Salvation Army shelter for the homeless. She dropped us off. I was stunned standing there with my wife and child in the snow watching my mother's car disappear into the frosty night. We checked in. At night they would allow us to use their facility, but during the day, we couldn't be there. It was awkward, embarrassing, and humbling.

The next day we went to the welfare office and started the ball rolling. We were going to get food stamps, and they would help us find a place to stay. It was all coming together. We actually stayed at the welfare office as long as we could because of the warmth. I dreaded going back out into the cold. I remember being really upset with my mother and me for allowing myself to be in this position. I didn't want to go back to my old ways. I really wanted to make a clean start and stay on the right side of the line, but I guess my circumstances were holding me back.

Back at the Salvation Army for the night, I watched as Regina lay our son down to sleep. She crawled in beside him, and as I tucked myself into my own bunk in the darkness of the dorm, I could hear Regina's crying herself to sleep. That really tore me up. I cried myself to sleep as well. Was I being the best father I could be? Was my son living the same life I did when I was his age? Was I letting my family down? I continued to cry, quietly.

When I woke up in the morning, I pondered where we were and how thankful I was for the Salvation Army and food stamps. I learned a lot over the past few nights. When my eyes opened to the new day, I was firm in my resolve. I vowed to never let my wife and son down again. I promised never to rely on my so-called family again. I had a plan, and the drive within me was growing. There was one thing I knew, and I knew it very well. The hustle was on and would be played at a whole new level. I would never be homeless again.

At first, things moved slowly. I was using food stamps and shelters, that is, until a kind couple took us in for a couple of weeks. I had never experienced such genuine generosity before. I was deeply touched. During my stay with them, I would venture into Columbus to work the streets, robbing drug dealers because they were a preferred target (they never reported the crime). I also shot dice, and I seldom lost. Money was starting to pile up and soon I had enough stashed to cover my rent in Newark, Ohio, for the next six months, with a little pocket change on the side. Once my family was settled into our apartment, I took my hustle into the next gear. Ohio was about to learn all about the hustler in me.

One day, I hooked up with my Uncle Victor's oldest son Pe Pe. He suggested that I consider moving to London, Ohio. There was more opportunity there for someone like me, and after all, my timing was perfect. People in Newark were getting to know me a little too well, especially after my latest confrontation at a bar's pool room. The owner of the club was a real nice black guy, but his brother was reckless. One day while I was playing a friendly game of pool with some guys, the owner's brother came up to me just as I was finishing up a game and bumped my arm, causing me to miss my shot and lose the game. I barked at him to be more careful next time. He swore, "F-you white boy. You don't need to be here. Go home!"

It amazed me how everyone thought of me as a white dude. Out of respect for this guy's brother, I decided to let it go. I ignored his remarks and turned to settle up with my pool opponent. All of a sudden I was grabbed from behind and held in a full nelson while being dragged outside of the bar. As soon as we were clear from the front door, I made my body go limp, allowing me to slide out of his hold on me. As I spun around, I noticed two things. One, a crowd was starting to gather around us and two, this knucklehead was standing in a fighter's stance. He actually wanted to duke it out with me. He continued to scream at me, as if it was supposed to scare me. Instead, I laughed as I leaned in towards him and delivered one shot to his mouth followed by three rapid shots to the head. He went down before he knew what hit him. I then jumped up and came slamming down, landing my foot only inches from his head. I turned to the crowd and yelled at them, "When he wakes up, I want you to tell him that I could have messed up his face real bad, but instead, I gave him a chance. I forgive him for his stupidity." With that, one of the guys I was playing pool with took my arm and pulled me out of there. It was over.

One day, a week or so after the knockout at the bar, the owner saw me and thanked me for sparing his brother's face. He told me that I was welcome back at his establishment anytime and promised that no one would try to bother me. I thanked him. He told me that, at first, after seeing what I did to his brother, he wanted to come and find me. Then, he heard from people what had really happened and how I actually spared his brother some serious facial damage. He respected my control. We remained friends from that day on. His brother avoided me all together.

1 Timothy 5:8

But if anyone does not provide for his relatives, and especially for members of his household, he has denied the faith and is worse than an unbeliever.

Chapter 9: Our Cups Overflowed

Because Regina and I were in need of a place to stay and not being one to turn down a good opportunity when I saw one, when Pe Pe offered us shelter at his place, we accepted. I was now able to put Newark, Ohio, behind me. There was finally a light shinning at the end of the tunnel I called my life.

Both Pe Pe and I enrolled at Millis Training Institute (M.T.I.) with dreams of becoming contributing members of society, that is, if society would have us. M.T.I. offered an intensive training course in truck mechanics, a field that drew my attention. Going to school together just seemed to make the entire experience more fun and easier. He motivated me and I him. We were a rock solid team.

In the morning, our ladies would cook breakfast while our kids would play. After eating and being entertained by the kids, we would kiss our ladies and head off to trucking school. It all seemed too perfect. Or was it?

These were very lean days. Being a full-time student didn't pay very well. Things were getting tight. We had to budget every penny with little or no room for error. If we overspent, there would be no food on the table. It was as simple as that. The writing was on the wall. We needed to come up with a solution, quickly. I even told Pe Pe what I knew to be an inevitability—we will have many hungry days ahead of us. Pe Pe was never one to worry about such things.

He liked to live on a day-by-day basis. Why worry about tomorrow when today is here, right there in front of you? My warnings landed upon deaf ears. The only person I could speak with and actually carry on a two-way conversation about our financial situation was Regina. She looked me square in the eye and with a firm tone to her voice replied, "Don't you go getting yourself in trouble now, and don't you get Pe Pe in any trouble either!"

I was at a loss for words. I reassured her that my bad boy days were behind me. I didn't think she was able to see the lie within my eyes.

As we left for school the next morning, I leaned over to Pe Pe and said, "Pe Pe, we're not going to school today. We need a break from our routine. All that money drama at home is depressing."

Pe Pe was kind of with me, but I'm not sure he fully understood. "Sure, whatever you say," he replied in an uncaring way.

I told him that we needed to have a serious one-on-one talk not his favorite thing to do. I was determined to pull Pe Pe out of his comfort zone, to have a man-to-man talk with him about our mutual financial situation. Instead of heading into Columbus, we went a different direction, towards a bar I knew in Newark. When we arrived, there was nobody there. Pe Pe and I had the place to ourselves. We entered the room in the rear and sat down with our large glasses of OJ. (it was too early for beer).

I asked Pe Pe if he was tired of fighting with his wife about money he didn't have. "Sure I am," he replied without adding any additional comment.

I continued, "Look at us. Here we are in the prime of our lives with families, and we are reduced to selling our blood to help pay for school and food." Just saying those words was making m

angry. It was as if I had a natural talent for preaching. I stood up
and while pacing back and forth, I continued, "Today is a new
day for you and me and for those we love. No longer will we be
considered regulars at the blood bank. No longer will we have to
worry about what we will or won't eat tonight. No longer will we
go to sleep at night, not knowing how we will make it through the
next day. Those days are gone!"

I swear, Pe Pe was almost up onto his feet ready to shout,
"Hallelujah." He was hanging on every word that spewed from my
lips. He believed everything I had to say, and so did I. I had a plan
and it was time to bring it forth. Pe Pe was all ears.

The first order of business was to teach Pe Pe a few of my
former cons. These were sure to immediately bring a little extra
pocket change. It took me only five minutes to teach him the
Number-On-The-Bill trick. After a few hours, Pe Pe was up to
speed on a number of my basic cons. He absorbed the details as
quickly as I delivered them. After lunch, we would put his learning
to the test.

Heading over to a nearby theater, I entered alone and proceeded
to the snack counter. I used my last and only $50 to purchase a
large popcorn and soda. Before paying, I wrote a phone number
on the bill and watched as the clerk rung up my sale on the cash
register. About 20 minutes later, Pe Pe came in and purchased a
small popcorn and paid for it with a five-dollar bill. Now, all of the
money we had to our name was gone. This better work!

Just as it had been when I was there earlier, the concession stand
was busy with dozens of people waiting to purchase snacks. As Pe
Pe took his change and started walking away, the next customer
stepped up to place his or her order. Pe Pe immediately came back

complaining that he was short-changed. The clerk said, "Sir, you paid with a five-dollar bill, and I gave you the proper change."

Pe Pe demanded that he paid with a 50-dollar bill and wanted to speak with a manger immediately. There was no sense arguing with the clerk. They don't have very much authority with these matters. When the situation was explained to the manager, the manager said that he was confident that his clerk was not in error. Pe Pe replied, "Look, I paid with a 50-dollar bill, and I can prove it. First of all, it was the only 50 I had and second, I had a friend's phone number written on it. I think the number started with 3-3-4."

The manager opened the till and after looking at the few 50 dollar bills, he saw the one with a phone number on it. It began with the numbers 3-3-4. The manager asked Pe Pe for the remaining numbers, and Pe Pe got angry yelling, "If I knew the number, why would I have written it down? Now stop wasting my time and give me back my 50!"

The bill was placed into Pe Pe's hand, and he quickly made his exit. As I left the theater and rounded the corner to our predetermined meeting place, I found Pe Pe sitting there laughing with excitement. Our minimal investment paid off big time. Many of my cons were that easy. We would eat well tonight.

Pe Pe and I had been going to school together for months without missing a day. Today, the one day we decided to play hooky was the one day that Pe Pe's wife came to the school to visit him. When we arrived at home, she was waiting for him with a cute smile upon her face. In the sweetest voice she asked how school was, and Pe Pe did the only thing that came natural to him, he lied. As he said the words, "School was fine," she bashed him one in the head. That was when the screaming started. Pe Pe bolted for the bathroom, locking the door behind him. This was literally the only place he could go where her reach was limited. She followed, banging on the bathroom door, yelling all kinds of obscenities at him. Regina and I stayed hidden in our room, laughing quietly to ourselves. We could clearly hear her accusing Pe Pe of cheating. She thought he was with another woman when in reality he was working to place food on their table. Go figure! I guess I can see where she was coming from. It did look suspicious. But all she had to do was talk to him in a calm, normal tone, and the fight would have been over as quickly as it started. Then again, Pe Pe shouldn't have lied.

Finally, I approached the battle zone and started explaining what we were up to and why we didn't go to school. She didn't believe me. Her accusations started coming my way, as if I were responsible for her man's infidelity. I even showed her the money we earned, but she still was over the edge with rage. It took her a couple of days to finally calm down. Her exaggerated angry demeanor seemed suspicious to me. It was as though she was hiding something, a dark little secret of her own. I kept my thoughts to myself. It was easier to keep the peace than stir the pot. From that day forward, Pe Pe and I would regularly work our cons and sometimes Pe Pe would venture off on his own. He was a quick study and in some ways I was proud of him, like any teacher is of their "A" student.

Finally, the day came when Pe Pe and I graduated from M.T.I. Pe Pe aced his exams, but I barely made it by the skin of my teeth. By now Regina and I were fed up living with the constant nagging. Poor Pe Pe! We felt sorry for him and the verbal abuse he had to endure. But then again that was Pe Pe's problem, not ours. It was time for us to move on. Being a M.T.I. graduate didn't guarantee us work. The problem with being a truck mechanic, when customers wanted work done on their $80,000 rig, they wanted only experienced mechanics, not some fresh out-of-school rookie, so work was scarce.

I relocated my family to Columbus, Ohio, on Say Avenue. I was going to miss living with Pe Pe but was glad to get as far away as I could from his nemeses of a wife. I was now living only a block away from Buck, a friend I met through Bama. Sadly, Bama passed away from heart failure, and at such a young age.

Buck and I became very close friends. Whenever I visited Buck's house, I would sneak some candy in for the boys. Buck's wife would ask me not to give them candy because after we would leave, the kids would go crazy on a sugar high. I guess I could see her point, but my memories of Uncle Nicky giving me money for candy as a young child were strong and enjoyable. I think deep down inside I wanted to be like Uncle Nicky to Buck's boys. None of us realized it at the time that Buck's kids, the boys I treated like my own, would grow up like I did, knowing the streets. They were to be the future leaders of the Short North Posse. They would remember me and my candy the same way I remembered Uncle Nicky.

As Buck and I talked about our mutual financial problems, I decided that I would offer a partnership to Buck, and if he was interested, we would soon both be living the high life. Buck was eager to earn more. Basically I told him that the weed in Ohio was below standard quality, so if we saved up enough money, we could go to New York and purchase two pounds for the price of one. Now in Ohio, if you purchased a 25-cent bag ($25 worth of pot), you barely got what you paid for. My plan was to create overflowing 25-cent bags. The repeat business would prove to be very profitable. When we pooled our financial resources, we came up with a grand total of $75, not exactly enough for the initial investment. That was when we were approached by a guy we knew who wanted to borrow $50. He offered to pay us back in two days with 50% interest attached. Hmmm, interesting concept. This was the birth of our loan sharking business.

Business was good and unlike the stereotypical loan sharks you hear about, Buck and I were real cool about it. At the end of the week, when we came collecting, we thanked our customers for their business. If they were a little short and couldn't pay off the loan, we just asked them for the interest, allowing the principal to ride for another week with compounded interest. It was a very lucrative situation. We never tried to strong-arm anyone to pay off their debt. In fact, when folks did pay off their remaining balance, we would ask them if they were sure they could afford it. Business was pretty good, except during tax time. When people got their refund checks, the first thing they would do was to settle their debts. The big money was in the compounded interest. A month after tax season, they would be broke again, back in line, asking us for another loan. The terms remained the same.

Pe Pe started showing up in Columbus more and more. I guess he was looking for a quiet retreat from his nagging wife. One day Pe Pe told me there was this guy who lived near Pe Pe's place. He was some sort of big shot Ohio underworld character who wanted to meet with me and Pe Pe to discuss a business opportunity. I was intrigued. I asked Pe Pe to set up the meeting. We ended up meeting with him at his house. I wasn't very pleased with the location, but

100   on the other hand, what was he going to do? Now I knew where he lived.

Before our sit down, I had some of my guys check him out. I wanted to know with whom I was dealing. It turns out he wasn't really a big shot. Instead, he was just a small-time hood trying to make it on his own. I could respect that. Just to be on the safe side, while I was sitting in this dude's living room being all nice and friendly, I had his house completely surrounded.

This short, little, hairy man had an idea for cashing fraudulent checks. He somehow got a hold of a series of blank checks from a certain company, and because he had an arrangement with the accountant, all we needed to do was travel around the country cashing them for a percentage cut in the profits. He wanted us to spend two weeks cashing these checks before disappearing off the map. The company's insurance would eat the losses. This was a clean white-collar crime where nobody got hurt, except for the big insurance companies. The only thing we had to be sure of was not to cash any of them in Ohio. I listened to what he had to say and told him I would have to think about it. When we left, my boys on lookout informed me that no suspicious activity was seen in or around the house during our meeting.

I really took my time in making a decision on the check scheme. My loan sharking business was doing well, and we were investing some of our profits into making purchases of New York weed. I wasn't really sure I needed any additional stress in my life. My plate was full. Pe Pe surprised me with his continued nagging. I think he was spending too much time with his wife. He was nagging at me to take the job, not only for myself but for him as well. He wanted to make his own mark, earn his own way so this job could be the stepping stone he needed to move up the ladder. I caved in and told him I would do it. Pe Pe and I started travelling around the country, cashing checks, but not staying in any one place too long. We were constantly on the move.

We decided to stop by and visit Claymont who was now living in Tallahassee, Florida. It had been a long time since we had seen each other, and time does heal old wounds. Claymont moved to Florida some time ago to escape the heat he was attracting around his building in Flatbush. The community was getting tired of the shootings, the drug dealers on every corner, and how dangerous their neighborhood had become. There were just too many gangsters hanging around Claymont's, which meant he was becoming a person of interest to all the wrong people. Claymont knew when it was time for him to leave. Florida seemed like a good place to plant himself, just until things cooled down up north.

I was surprised at how beautiful Claymont's Florida house was. Everything was first class. The décor was tropical and inviting. I was very comfortable there. *I could live like this*, I thought to myself. The drinking, bragging, and exaggerating were as free flowing from me as from everybody there. It got to the point where I didn't know what to believe. This went on nonstop for a couple of days. The hangover finally grounded me with reality. It was time to say goodbye to Claymont and make the trek north, all the way to Ohio. My mission here was done.

When I returned home, I was pleased to see that all was well with my family, with my friends, and of course, with my business. Buck did a great job running things as I knew he would. He managed things like a real pro. The loan sharking revenues were peaking. I think Buck may have missed his calling. If he had stayed in school

102 and worked towards his degree, he would have made an amazing loan officer. These were truly profitable days, our cups overflowed.

Job 16:3

Will your long-winded speeches never end? What ails you that you keep on arguing?

Chapter 10: Heavy Metal

One day Buck came up to me and told me that there was someone he wanted me to meet. Her name was Lady Snake, and she rode with a group of bikers known as Heavy Metal. This exclusive motorcycle club was primarily black, unlike the stereotypical white clubs you see on television. Lady Snake didn't live very far from my place, so I agreed to go to her place with Buck, as long as it didn't take too much time. We had an informative conversation with both of us being equally curious about the other. During our conversation, a rather tall and heavy set looking man entered the room. At first, I was alarmed, but with quick introductions, I was back feeling at ease. His name was Magic and he was Lady Snake's old man. He just sat there listening with a big smile on his face while his woman and I carried the brunt of the conversation. I was positive that they were interested in me for my pot. Why else would strangers be so nice? Not once did weed come into the conversation.

Magic was the club's national vice president, and when I asked him if he wanted to smoke a joint, he politely declined. He told me that he didn't smoke or get drunk because of his responsibilities, but insisted that I go ahead and light up if I wanted to. I admired him for his conviction, so I did not fire up a joint.

Buck and I were invited to join Lady Snake and Magic at their club for an evening of socializing. I really liked these people. We agreed to meet them at the club at 7 p.m. Once I walked into the clubhouse that evening, I felt like I was at home. I belonged here. All of the people I met were deep down good people. I started hanging out with the Heavy Metal Motorcycle Club more and more. Being almost white and not riding a bike made me feel like I was sticking out like a sore thumb, and I was. They would laugh when I showed up, knowing I arrived on four wheels instead of two.

I needed to blend in more and quickly. The last thing I wanted was to be adopted into this group with a nickname like "Four Wheels" or "Auto." Most of my time there was spent asking questions about motorcycles: Which ones were fast? Which ones offered comfort? Extended forks looked cool but meant sacrificing turning radius. Remove the baffles and you could be heard approaching from almost a mile away. Magic and Lady Snake also gave me personal lessons on how to drive a bike. Shifting with your feet and braking with a foot and hand at the same time was a challenge. But as I said earlier, I was always a quick study. Yes, I was getting the itch. It was time for me to become an easy rider. I bought a bike with the help of my new friends. They all had an opinion to share, thinking what they had to say was more important than what anyone else thought. I absorbed all of their wisdom and ended up making a decision that worked for me. I bought a fast bike that was not only comfortable to ride but also maneuverable and within my budget. I was becoming one of them, and I liked it. I felt cool.

More and more I was shown around Columbus, visiting the other black biker clubs, each with a unique name of their own. I never knew these hangouts existed. I was impressed. There was even a club named the Eagles, made up primarily of all the older bikers. These were the guys you went to when you needed some advice. These guys had decades of experience under their belts and no one allowed it to go to waste. In my circle, I was the one who usually had to hand out the advice. I was considered the older and wiser one, but compared to these guys, I was a freshman.

Not all the clubs were black. There were a couple of clubs that we would visit where most of the members where white. Sure there would be a couple of black guys too, but they were definitely the minority. Interestingly enough, race didn't seem to matter. The common bond was the bike and the colors worn, worn like a flag, worn with pride. I understood what these things meant. I was familiar with the concept of family. It reminded me of the Mau Maus and all of my uncles. I missed them a lot.

One day while visiting a group of Viet Nam Vet bikers, I witnessed exactly how these guys stuck together. One of the dudes suddenly started freaking out, throwing beer bottles around, and swearing at everyone in his sight, including me. Did anyone get pissed off or try to take this crazy man down? No! Instead a bunch of guys gathered around him and spoke with soothing voices. Within moments the room was filled with calm as they all embraced in what looked like the biggest group hug I had ever seen. I found out later that the poor guy was experiencing a flashback to the jungles in Viet Nam where his buddies were being killed right next to him as their position was overrun by the enemy. Once again, the Viet Nam Vets demonstrated the depths of the family bond. What irritated me the most was how we—Americans—shouted slurs at the Viet Nam Vets as they came home. Where was the love? Where was the respect? Where was the support?

I remember one night while I was minding my own business

when someone had the balls to ask me why I hung out with so many black bikers. At first, I was shocked but soon composed myself to where I could provide an honest answer. I started to explain about the meaning of family, not the family you are born into but instead the family who cares for you and dies for you. I ran down a list of names of those I considered to be my brothers, and most were black. I went on to say that I didn't even see color when I see people, a trait that I wished all people could exercise. But sadly enough, just like this guy asking me that stupid question, color was all they saw. I was getting irritated once again. For me, I guess it came down to one simple truth: I hung out with people who made me feel comfortable. I never felt comfortable in the same room with a racist.

The topic of my selling pot finally did come up with Magic, and to my surprise, he had no problem with my conducting business on his club's premises. Once Magic said it was okay to buy my weed the customers seemed to line up. I wondered if Magic wanted to get to know me so he could bring in a decent supply line of weed for his guys. If so, that was fine by me. Everyone buying from me got great deals, bags overflowed. The days of not finding someone to buy pot from were long gone. I was always there. I was now a regular supplier.

Without my knowing it, the bikers took a vote. They were putting it to the membership to see if they wanted me to become one of their "Probes." Being welcomed in their group as a Probe was the first step to climbing the ladder and becoming a ranking officer. There wasn't one single vote that was against me. It was now official. Being a Probe meant that I would have to do any crappy job I was asked to do, as long as the request came from full patch member. I couldn't be asked to do anything illegal or to do work at someone's home. I felt honored. The Probe position would last a full ninety days, similar to Hell Week in the Marines, except my Hell Week would last for three months. I was up to the challenge.

As time passed, I took on more and more responsibilities. I began running the club on Thursday night (ladies' night). By this time, Pe Pe and his nagging wife had split up. It was about time. I found out later they broke up because the nag was sleeping with the same want-a-be gangster who had us cashing those blank checks. Small world!

Pe Pe realized that this was his opportunity for freedom to meet women. There were not only better fish in the sea, but there were also nicer fish as well. He would miss seeing his kids everyday. Pe Pe's ex-wife poisoned their minds against their dad. I guess you can say she nagged the love right out of them. Ladies' night was a good time for Pe Pe to explore his new freedom. I was happy for him.

With Pe Pe now working with Buck and me, it was easy enough to show them how I wanted things to go. "You don't sell weed to civilians. Keep them for the loan sharking business," I would teach. I added, "Selling to bikers is the safest way to make money. Keep these guys happy, and they will always be there for you. Sometimes it's beneficial to have one (or six) bikers next to you."

Pe Pe and Buck learned quickly. I was responsible for everything that went on at the club and had to answer for the times when things didn't go very well. I was accountable.

Now that I was working and climbing the corporate ladder, I felt that it was time to make the move, to make things with me and Regina permanent. I asked her to marry me, and without hesitation, she said yes. We selected a date and the arrangements were solidified. Regina took care of most of the wedding business while I continued to work the club and manage my other business interests. I couldn't believe it. I was going to get married. Regina glowed.

One my wedding day, Pe Pe was nowhere to be found. I would have liked him to be there but no worries, Buck was my best man. We could do this thing without Pe Pe. The day started out with good intentions, but circumstances continued to get in my way. Yes, I was late for my own wedding. Buck picked me up early in the morning, and all we had to do was make one quick stop along the way. We allowed 30 minutes for this stop but ended up needing much more time. We had a customer who borrowed some money from us a long time ago. He had paid his interest payments regularly but refused to settle up on the principle. Finally, the day came when he felt that he had paid enough in interest. He thought that since his interest payments now far exceeded the amount of the original loan, there was no reason for us to continue bleeding him. Buck and I were going to stop by his place and explain to him the terms of the loan. This wasn't going to be a debate either. He wasn't home. Also, he was not at his store (the store he set up with the money borrowed from me). Just as we were about to give up, Buck got a call from someone informing us that this deadbeat was hanging out at an apartment on the southside of Columbus.

As we approached, we saw our guy sitting on the trunk of a car, visiting with a couple of other dudes. None of these guys were slight in stature. We parked and walked towards them. My customer stood facing us, as if he was going to do something stupid. Before he could make a move or say a word, I slapped him. You could see the shock overtake him and his friends. Before anything could be said, I pulled out my .38 and shoved the barrel into his mouth. "Where's my money?" I demanded. No answer. His mouth was full. We threw him into the trunk of our car and sped off down the road towards a little more secluded spot. We intentionally hit every bump along the way. Now don't get me wrong, my goal was to scare this fool, and scare him I did. Most gangsters of that day would have simply popped him one and dumped the body under a slab of concrete somewhere. However, dead people don't pay back their debts. Since I am not a killer, and never wanted to be, it was my objective to use more reasonable means of persuasion. After having a nice one-on-one chitchat with the guy in my trunk, we let him go to think about the error of his ways. I had my complete payment within two days. I laughed about the fact that the same guy came to me six months later to borrow more cash. The terms remained the same, and he understood. I never had problems with him again.

Buck and I arrived 45 minutes after the wedding ceremony was due to start; we noticed they were all waiting. They all knew my business and were not surprised at my tardiness. First order of business was to walk around, greet everyone and thank them for making the journey to witness my big day. In attendance were Uncle Victor, my sister Madeline and her husband Chuck, my favorite cousin Steve, Mymysala, Hazel (Regina's mother, who flew in from New York), my mother and Jose. I was blessed with two best men: Buck and my son Louis, Jr., who was now two years old. It was all so perfect.

Instead of hosting a reception, we simply went back to Buck's girlfriend's house and laughed, danced, and celebrated as a family. It was a special day for Regina and me. The fun continued until the nighttime gave way to the day. All day I bragged to Regina about how I was going to make love to her. The magical honeymoon moment finally arrived. She was ready, and so was I. As she disappeared into the bathroom to prepare herself, I too got ready for the perfect ending of the perfect day. I lay in bed, resting my head upon my pillow. When Regina returned, was she greeted with my sensual desire? No, instead she was greeted by my snoring. I was in a deep sleep and wasn't going to wake up until many hours later. Regina would never let me live that one down. She would joke about our wedding night for decades.

These were good, profitable times. I was a firm believer in sharing the wealth, so I had no fears of people's snitching on us to the cops. Now and then, the law would try to pin something on me, but no charges were ever filed. We were just pot pushers, no threat to anyone. For the most part, we were left alone and that was the way I liked it. People continued to borrow money from us even though we had a reputation of doing bad things to those who broke the rules. It's funny how fast and far rumors will travel when it is regarding something mean and ugly. But do the rumors spread about how many times we gave someone a break or helped them out of a financial jam? Never! Oh well, I slept well at night.

One family who borrowed from us actually spoke to the cops about our little loan shark business. A couple of detectives came out to speak with me, but they really had nothing on me, so there wasn't much they could do. Perhaps my clients were simply trying to get out of their financial obligation to me. These folks were truly paranoid. They were afraid of their own shadow. In their minds, everyone was out to get them, to do them harm. Nevertheless, they did settle their debts, but still the cops had us in their sights. We were now in that uncomfortable place, above the radar. I didn't like it there. The timing of events always amazed me. This was the same time that Claymont called me from Florida to see if I could spare a few guys to head south and help him out with his new club. Next stop: Tallahassee.

Ephesians 5:11

*Take no part in the unfruitful works of darkness,
but instead expose them.*

Chapter 11: A General in the Devil's Army

A meeting was arranged at my house to determine who would go to Florida to help Claymont and who would stay behind to keep an eye on things in Ohio. The last thing I wanted was for my business interest to suffer while helping Claymont. Since the cops were watching us, waiting for someone to make that one stupid mistake that would land us in prison, I needed to make sure the person left behind was smart enough to stay out of jail and bold enough to handle our business growth. A few names were suggested, but those guys didn't impress me enough for me to bank it all on their ability. They just weren't old school. I also worried about their loyalty if they were busted. Would they keep their mouths shut, or would they sing like little birdies? It was decided that the executive branch of the Heavy Metals would handle things while Pe Pe, Buck, and I headed south. It was going to be a short-term arrangement.

I told Regina that I would send for her once I found an apartment and got settled in. She agreed. I could tell that she was a little nervous, but for the most part, she had faith in her husband and his abilities. She knew it would all work out, or at least that was her prayer. After packing up the car with food and enough alcohol to last the journey, Pe Pe, Buck, and I started our 15-hour drive south.

I always enjoyed road trips. Before we knew it, we were parking the car beneath a swaying palm tree, a sight you never

114 see up north in Ohio. I stood there for a few minutes taking it all in—the warmth of the breeze dancing across my face, the sounds of laughter coming from a nearby park, the smells. I especially remember enjoying the sweet, inviting, tropical scents.

After unpacking the car at Claymont's house, we were given a tour of his new club. While looking around and assessing the task at hand, I asked Claymont what happened to all of the help he had when Pe Pe and I were there the last time. He explained that one guy, the club's manager, was constantly making passes at his wife. "Dumb career move," I commented. The other workers were caught stealing from the till, so he had no other option but to fire them all. I soon learned the truth through the rumor mill. It was actually Claymont who was making passes at the manager's wife and the employees quit because of the back pay situation. That sounded a lot more like something Claymont would do. It all started making sense now. Nevertheless, we were hired to do a job, so I preferred keeping all that personal stuff in the closet. There was no mixing business with pleasure, especially if you wanted to be successful.

Now that we had an idea of the scope of Claymont's needs, we sat down and pulled together a business plan. Buck was put in charge of the disco and Pe Pe would manage the Oyster Bar. My job would be to oversee the entire operation, which meant that I was the one to carry the stress of making connections with local drug dealers. We reopened the club with a huge week-long grand opening celebration. We attracted a large crowd from three of the nearby colleges. The daytime operation offered across-the-board discounts and in the evening, ladies got in for free. We were at max capacity almost every night. Claymont was blown away. He knew

he made the right decision when he called the Ohio boys for help.
We all profited.

I had to enforce a strict policy that assured us that any drugs
being sold on these premises would be our drugs. In that way, we
were guaranteed to receive a cut, the first and biggest cut. All the
dealers agreed and things started coming together like a well-oiled
machine. Pe Pe would spend his shift socializing with the clients
at his Oyster Bar, having a great time. He was actually drawing in
business. I was pleased. Buck enjoyed music and so putting him
in charge of the disco was a good choice. He was a natural for the
job. He insured there would be no trouble on his floor and balanced
Donna Summer and the Bee Gees with just enough Latino music
to keep the dance floor hopping. For me, I just kept running around
like a chicken without its head, making sure things continued
running smoothly. They did!

One guy who wanted to sell pot in our club approached me
with a business proposition. He knew I was running things for
Claymont, and he was the one guy I tried to hook up with earlier,
without success. He was the main dude who ran the pot business in
this part of town. He was hired by someone who not only trusted
him but also gave him protection as part of his job description.
I had to make an impression, one that would establish a mutual
friendship and trust. I allowed him to speak first. He was interested
in setting up a contact guy in our club to sell pot to our customers.
He followed with an assurance that we, the management, would
see a cut from the profits. Before he could say another word, I
interrupted, "Are you out of your freakin' mind?"

I didn't wait for his answer. As his mouth opened to utter his
reply I continued, "I tell you what. You sell us the pounds at a

reasonable price, and we won't go looking elsewhere for our pot needs. Plus, you won't have to deal with the risk of getting busted!"

He took the deal. It was settled with a handshake. We would make the lion's share of profits, and that was what counted. Yes, I could have told him to kiss my ass, but this was his territory and by making a solid business relationship with him, I was also establishing a relationship with his employer and the protection that came along with it. It was a good business decision.

You would think it was "Spring Break" by the number of cars that jammed our parking lot. These crazy kids were actually sleeping in their cars to insure they weren't too far from the party going on inside the club. We hired someone to cook breakfast at the Oyster Bar, just to make sure those sleeping outside didn't spend any money elsewhere for their eggs and OJ. This arrangement did interfere with Pe Pe's routine at first. After all, Pe Pe was there from 5 a.m. until 2 a.m. the next morning. He survived on only three hours sleep, if that. Seeing the Oyster Bar being taken over by a breakfast cook was somewhat irritating to Pe Pe, and he wasn't shy about making his opinion known. We sat down and looked at the situation from all angles. When Pe Pe realized that he didn't actually have to work in the Oyster Bar, but instead simply be there as a department head, he began to relax. Opening the doors in the morning and locking up at closing time were the most critical part of his responsibilities. Having his breakfast cooked for him every morning started to make a lot more sense. Pe Pe adapted well, as we all did.

The first month seemed to take years to end. It was now time for me to head back to Ohio to gather up my family. I was excited about how I knew Regina would love Florida, but most of all, I was excited about seeing my wife and son. I missed them terribly. When I first arrived back in Ohio and glanced at my family, my eyes started filling with tears of joy. It was an amazing time; our anticipation and adrenaline drove us all the way back down to Florida. I was right; Regina did fall in love with Florida even though we both knew this to be a temporary stay. We settled into an apartment only a few blocks from the club. This was handy since I spent 80% of my day working. It was easy for Regina to stop by if she wanted to see me. I was always glad to see her, especially when she brought Louis Junior with her. If Regina ever needed anything, she knew she could call or come over. She was my priority, not Claymont.

One sunny afternoon, I got a call from Regina. She was somewhat upset about not having any food in the house. I dropped what I was doing, and within minutes, I was home handing my wife $300 so she could go grocery shopping. She knew she could count on me, and once again, I proved that point by accepting her invitation to join her at the supermarket. As we headed out the door, I couldn't help thinking to myself, *Okay, wise guy. What did you get yourself into?*

I followed her like a lost puppy. I had no idea of what I was doing. I never compared prices or looked at expiration dates, and most of all, I was totally embarrassed trying to figure out coupons. I think most men would understand, at least in those days.

Walking up and down the aisle, I was putting food into the cart, food that I thought we needed and food that made sense to me. Regina had her own agenda and by time we reached the checkout counter, our cart was literally overflowing. The final tally came to $423. That was $123 over our $300 budget. Watching Regina and the check out girl remove unneeded items to get the total down by $123, I was overcome with embarrassment. I slithered away to the security of my car and waited. I left it to Regina to figure it out, even though she was equally embarrassed by the situation. She never asked me to help her do grocery shopping again. I was all right with that.

These were good times: plenty of money to be made, that is, until the dry spell hit town. The bad times snuck up on us without warning. The beginning of the bad times started when we were almost killed by a bunch of angry Cubans. They just drove up to the club and screeched to a stop within a few yards from our front door. Two guys jumped out with submachine guns and opened fire, spraying everything in front of them with bullets, hundreds of bullets. They left as quickly as they arrived.

Buck, Pe Pe, and I were hiding deep inside, behind the bar for the 60 seconds it took for them to run out of ammo. When it was over, we all looked at each other and without a word being said, we simultaneously broke out into laughter. This was our way of handling the near-death fear that was still lingering within us. "You see," I started to bark, "That's why we don't get involved with crack. That crap will make you crazy."

Pe Pe and Buck were in agreement. Together, we slowly made our way from our hiding place to have a look around. We needed to assess the damage, and there was plenty. Obviously these Cubans were from Miami. Our club was the sweetest one in Tallahassee and because of that we drew all kinds of attention, especially from the Cubans. Florida was their turf, but I just wanted everyone to get along. Florida was a pretty big pie and there were enough pieces for everyone. Too bad not everyone shared my point of view.

The damage was extensive. The cops would have to be involved. Many store windows were shot out as well as every car parked in front of the club. Even the street signs looked as if they belonged in a war zone. Not one person was hurt. Just goes to show you how careless random shooting can be. Up north, if gangsters wanted you dead, they would walk up to you and pop you one. You and you alone would be taken out, not innocent people nearby, although there were some exceptions to that rule.

These Cuban thugs wanted to make sure their message was received. It was. When they called Claymont asking for a sit down meeting, I was the one who was recruited to handle the negotiations. I wasn't very pleased with that, but I had my responsibilities. A job is a job. I took Buck with me, along with a car load of guys from my crew. We were armed with anything we could carry. I wished we had an SMG (sub machine gun). This wasn't going to be like the old days when a rumble would erupt when negotiations went sour. This was going to be a blood bath if a mutual agreement couldn't be found. I wasn't ready to take a life. I would never be ready to do that!

We agreed to meet in a public place where all parties would feel safe. A local restaurant was selected. Buck and I made my way to the door, and my crew scattered outside finding locations where they could hunker down with a clear line of sight. Buck and I had no illusions about what we were walking into. We could have just as easily said goodbye to Claymont and took off for Ohio, but instead, we honored our obligation. Brothers to the death, right?

Buck and I both carried a couple of guns wishing we wouldn't have to use them. Seeing that both Buck and I had some military experience, and we were both somewhat crazy, if things went bad inside, I was confident that we would be able to shoot our way out of there. I had to believe that!

The conversation between me and the person I thought was in charge of their interest was heated. Swearing and yelling was being offered by both sides. It was getting so heated up I was expecting a gun battle to erupt at any minute. Even the waitress stayed as far away from us as she could. I didn't even know what they wanted at this point. I assumed that they were trying to take over the club, so my job was to prevent that from happening. I was certain by the end of this day I would be considered a murderer, even though it would have been in self-defense. Then, suddenly a man burst out of the kitchen speaking Spanish to my aggressive counterpart. I didn't let them know that I spoke fluent Spanish. I assumed they thought I was just some white guy. When the man from the kitchen told the thug I was arguing with to shut up, the thug obeyed. The boss ordered them to make a deal, not to fight. I glanced over towards Buck and by the look on my face he knew that things were going to be all right. There would be no blood bath today. I would go to sleep tonight a drug dealer, a hustler, and a gangster, but not a murderer.

Apparently their beef was not with us but instead with the people who ran the territory. We were just a business who got caught up in the middle of the local gang wars. We had no ties to anyone other than ourselves and with that we were able to form new alliances when needed.

The guy who came from the kitchen motioned for me to join him at another table. I did. He told me about the territory struggle his people were having. He also mentioned that he knew who I was and where I came from. He knew about my Puerto Rican background and also knew that I spoke Spanish. He laid it all on the table. I listened, nodding now and then in agreement. I was wondering if he knew about my small army hidden outside. The conversation got around to the crack business. He told me that this new drug was the wave of the future, and if we didn't get onboard, we would be ruined in no time. Pot would not support us anymore. I was agreeing with everything he had to say. Then he said something that surprised me. He told me that Claymont was a piece of shit, a real scumbag that couldn't be trusted. Again, I agreed with what I was hearing. I wasn't hearing anything that I could argue with. He continued telling me about a meeting they had with Claymont, but no agreement could be reached. Claymont was just too greedy.

Their warning to me was not to trust anything Claymont said. Buck, Pe Pe, and I were not in Claymont's future business plan. We were expendable. These Cubans simply wanted to send me a message and to Claymont too. For Claymont, the message was that "greed is not good for your health." For me, their message was "Do you really think my guys all have lousy aim? They didn't shoot you for a reason. Our argument is not with you. Go home!"

I had a lot to think about including my wife and son. These Cubans wanted the club and Claymont was throwing us under the bus. This club would be a great place for their crack business, but as long as I was there, it would remain crack free. I flashed back to the days when I watched my uncles getting high on heroin, the crack of those days. It wasn't a pretty sight. Seeing needles hanging from my Uncle Victor's arm was part of the reason I selected the path I was on. Yes, I sold heroin before, but only to junkies in gangs. I never wanted to be responsible for ruining a life, for causing such a slow and ugly death.

As our conversation ended, his hand was extended to me. I accepted it. He wanted to know what I was going to do, so I told him that I had a lot to think about. I promised to call. He gave me his direct number, but he knew by the look on my face no call would come. The meeting was over, and we all went on our way. For the next three weeks, business picked up and we had no signs of trouble from anyone, especially the Cubans. Crack houses started popping up in the neighborhood. The Cuban gang decided to use crack houses instead of muscling us at the club. Crack addicts who used to come to our club stopped coming altogether. They had a new place to play (and pay). I was 100% okay with that. "Let them kill themselves somewhere else," I laughed. My prediction came to pass. The neighborhood with all its crack houses went downhill, fast.

The club's business did suffer. Nobody wanted our weed anymore. Things were getting more and more depressed. One day Buck came up to me and said he wanted to return to Ohio. I didn't blame him. I was also contemplating my own exit strategy. We were having a hard time paying our rent. I didn't want to go back to the days when I had to worry about putting food on the dinner table. I sent Regina and my son back home to stay with my mother. I moved in with Claymont and Pe Pe. Pe Pe was worried about going back to Ohio. He thought his ex-wife was trying to have him put in jail; her residual nagging was still having an effect on poor Pe Pe.

Now you might ask why I stayed with Claymont all this time. Why I didn't head out of Tallahassee the first chance I had? I had plenty of opportunity to leave, but one thing kept me there

by Claymont's side: he was dying. Apparently he became H.I.V.
positive while volunteering to give a blood transfusion to a dying
woman years earlier. That day when he tried to give life, he ended
up taking two lives—hers and his. Eventually the doctor told me
that he had very little time left. To me, it just didn't seem right
that someone should die alone. For the few weeks Claymont had
remaining, I would be there to help him into the next life, wherever
that would be.

The day came when Claymont finally passed, peacefully. I was
the only one there by his side. I was the last person he saw before
closing his eyes for the last time. The world would not mourn for
this man. No one would. Not even I. Except for that lady he offered
his lifeblood to, he was a very bad man who had little concern for
others. He had robbed, and yes, killed many people in his day. That
was nothing to be proud of. If there was a God, then Claymont
would have a lot of explaining to do. Chances are he never made
it up that high. People like Claymont have only one place to spend
their eternity: Hell. Even though he was a bad man, I knew one
thing for sure. If I hadn't come along, there would have been so
many more people killed by this man's hand. I was able to keep
him and his lust for aggression reeled in. His life was that of a true
gangster, like you see in the movies. He was a man with no heart,
general in the Devil's Army.

2 Timothy 2:26

*And that they may come to their senses and escape the snare of
the Devil, having been taken captive by him to do his will.*

Chapter 12: The Dark Side Kept Calling My Name

Now that Claymont was resting six feet under, there was really nothing holding me back in Florida. It was finally time for me to return to those I loved, to the life I once had in the frigid north. I was Ohio bound. Claymont's funeral was without incident or tears. I would have expected his wife to show a little more appreciation for all I had done, but there was nothing there. She demonstrated no compassion, no love, no mourning—nothing. She was as frigid as Claymont's dead body. Claymont's house was an emotional empty nest from long before I arrived, so why should his passing make any difference? I was offered nothing for my services, companionship, and faithfulness—not a dime. I really didn't care. I wasn't interested in receiving blood money. But an offer would have been nice. At least that would have given me an opportunity to decline and walk away knowing I did the right thing. I still walked away feeling pretty good about my devotion to a real screwed up guy, right to the end. Till death do us part, remember?

Arriving home without a penny to my name, I convinced my mother to allow me and my family to stay with her just until I could line my pockets with cash once again. I didn't plan on living with her for very long. This was the last place Regina wanted to be, but as always, she stood by her man. Regina took one, again, for the team.

After one week of hustling, I had enough for the first month's

126 rent at our new apartment. We couldn't move from my mother's quick enough. I also landed a job at a nearby sandwich shop. It was a great place to work and had plenty of benefits. Even though I continued to hustle now and then, I was trying to stay as honest as I could. I really wanted to become a normal, everyday man-on-the-street citizen and leave all that violence and drug business behind me, locked away where I would never have to look at it again. I'll tell you this, after living the high life for such a long time, working for minimal wages was a difficult adjustment. The temptations were strong and constant.

Pe Pe returned to Ohio as well, but never settled down to one place. He kept on the move, stopping by every now and then just to let me know he was all right. I appreciated that. He was paranoid about the Fed's catching up with him and busting him for the check cashing deal we did years ago. I tried to explain to him that he was protected by the statute of limitations, but he preferred to live like a night crawler, staying alert, watching from deep within the shadows. I can't live like that.

My manager at the sandwich shop was a slim, white lady named Kay. Her boyfriend Richard was somewhat psycho, driven to near madness by uncontrollable jealousy. He was the sandwich shop's regional manager and a student at Ohio State. He had so much going for him, yet he was constantly dealing with the demons in his head. The demons were winning the battle. When Richard saw me working with Kay during one of his many trips to our shop, his jealousy pushed any remaining signs of sanity out of the picture. The fact that I was a Puerto Rican didn't help matters; in fact, it made things worse. There was no way I was going to come out ahead. I never did have the chance to put his mind at ease. White

girls just didn't do it for me. Yes, Kay and I got along really well, in
a very professional manner. She was my boss and I her employee,
just the way we both wanted it. A friendship blossomed between
us. Kay would open up about problems most employers wouldn't
share with an employee, but I have always been a good listener.
She just needed a shoulder to cry on, and I was willing to listen.
I made suggestions as to how she could deal with her stresses. I
knew she listened to some of my advice; she told me so. If only
that nutcase she was dating would listen to me as well, a lot of
anger and pain would have been avoided.

Just like everything else I do, I put 110% of my energy into
my work. I wanted to be the best, and I was. I took pride in myself
and what I did, and this showed in how I carried myself. Being
Latino wasn't always easy in Ohio. I knew all too well what it
was like for a black person to live the South. I was constantly
judged by the color of my skin, even though I was a white-skinned
Latino. A minority is a minority, regardless of his or her hue. It
was predetermined by just looking at me that I was an uneducated,
no good, hide-your-valuables-before-I-kill-you kind of bum. Yes,
I was a bad boy in many ways, but I did have common sense and
scruples. I was a man of honor. Treat me with respect, and I will
bend over backwards for you, regardless of the color of your skin.
Screw with me and I will show you how venomous my sting can
be.

Even though I was trying to keep my life clean and on the
straight and narrow, I continued to keep my ties with the Heavy
Metal Motorcycle Club. I had a strong bond with these brothers, so
seeing them helped me deal with all the other crap in my life such
as working for peanuts and avoiding Kay's boyfriend. Richard was

128 spending his time plotting against me, and one day he decided it was time to hatch his plan. Of course, he came to the shop on a day that Kay was off. He knew he would find me there. I was regular like clockwork. By now he had been introduced to my wife and son, but that didn't help things. He was convinced that I was cheating on my wife with Kay. There was no getting into that cement block of a skull of his. I wasn't going to change his opinions.

Entering the shop on Kay's day off, Richard asked me to go to another sandwich shop on the northside of town. He explained that they were busy and needed help. What was I going to do, tell the district manager no? Kay was grooming me for a management position within the organization and that meant more money and benefits for my family. A new store was being built in Reynoldsburg, and if I played my cards right, that store would be mine. I had too much to lose, so I agreed to go, as instructed.

When I arrived, I noticed that the store was quiet. There was only one customer eating a meal, and the manager was busy doing prep work while his one other employee swept the floors. I couldn't understand why I was needed here. My shop was a lot busier, and the lunch time crowd was only a few hours away. But who am I to argue with management? I approached the manager and reported in for duty. He was surprised to see me. The phone rang and so I waited for the manager to return. I was starting to think that I was being tested by upper management. I assumed they wanted to see how adaptable I was to change. That thought vanished when the manager returned, took me in the back, gave me a bucket and a toothbrush, and instructed me to sanitize all of the baseboards. I obeyed. I really wanted to hit him square in the jaw, but I swallowed my pride and did as I was told. Within

30 minutes, Richard entered the shop, walked right past me, and had a nice chitchat with the manager. I watched out of the corner of my eye as they both glanced my way, laughing at their private joke—me! I was never so humiliated in my life. That was the most degrading thing I ever had to endure. It took me all day to finish those baseboards, even though they looked clean before I started. I went home angry, hurt, and embarrassed. However, when I reached the comforting welcome of my wife and son, I was content. Regina asked, "How was your day?"

I smiled and swallowed my pride as I replied, "It was fine. How was yours?"

I would dream about meeting Richard and introducing him to my baseball bat. That thought made me laugh.

The next day at work, Richard came to take Kay out for lunch. Apparently they were going to have a business lunch, but I knew that they were just going to have a meal somewhere and submit the bill as part of their expenses. Before they left, Richard approached me bragging about the karate competition he had just competed in. He was going on and on about being a brown belt. This maggot was actually trying to intimidate me. I so desperately wanted to break out laughing, but instead, I held it in and tried to look as interested in his words as I could. That was really hard to do. Richard really thought he was the world's gift to martial arts. I wanted to introduce him to my baseball bat, the equalizer. I remembered my dream and gently smiled.

Every time Regina and Louis Junior would visit me at work, Kay offered them a sandwich and soda on the house. Today was no different. I was the one who got to prepare the meal for them, and brought sheer joy to my soul to see my son watching his daddy

130   work, preparing something tasty for him. That boy loved to eat. As they took their meal and headed to an empty seat by the front window, Richard's worker friend noticed Regina and Louis Junior receiving a free meal. He came up to me and said, "What did those two monkeys want?" Then he broke out into laughter.

Regina always told me to hold my temper when this sort of thing happens. As you know by now, I had anger management issues. This guy had no idea who I was. To him, I was just another employee doing slave labor. Because he was a friend of Richard's, he walked around with an air of pomposity. The thought of how white folks usually wait until a black person is out of hearing range before speaking narrow-minded slurs added to the anger boiling up inside me. With one full-force punch to his mouth, I placed this bigot on the floor. It was nap time for him. On his way down to the floor, he travelled some distance backwards, knocking over everything in his path. That felt really good.

Kay, who was in the back taking care of administrative paper work, came running out to see what was going on. From the look on her face, I knew I was in trouble. Somebody called the police and within minutes the emergency squad came flooding into the shop. I was pushed against the wall, frisked, and immediately handcuffed. The bigot was still napping.

Richard soon showed up and that was when I first realized that I was going to lose my job. I tried to explain to everyone what happened, but nobody would listen. Only Kay showed signs of understanding, but the deed was done, and the chain of events was soon out of her hands. She wouldn't get a say in my disposition.

As I was being formerly arrested, the police sergeant who approached me recognized me from the Rick Moore Academy a local martial arts facility. I had recently started spending my spare time developing an interest in structured combat. I loved the discipline and especially loved watching the fights. I once told the national president of the Iron Dragons that I was interested in learning more about martial arts. Since he was a martial arts' master and because we rode motorcycles together, he agreed to take me to meet Master Moore at the Rick Moore Academy to see if there was any way I could be taught at an accelerated rate. I was an accomplished street fighter and extremely cocky. Looking at this skinny man they called Master Moore, I thought to myself, "What can this guy teach me that I didn't already know?"

Master Moore must have read my mind. He invited me to the mat. He and his technique were amazing. No matter how I tried to defend myself, the floor was being wiped with my body. I was flung and dragged from one end of the dojo (training hall) to the other. The master could have injured me at any time, but instead he taught me a very valuable lesson. I grew the deepest respect for the martial arts that day. A passion developed that would influence how I would spend the rest of my life.

Because the sergeant recognized me from that day in the dojo (he was a black belt who trained with Master Moore), he pulled me aside and asked me to explain to him what happened. I went into detail about making my family a free lunch, a common practice approved by Kay. Then I went on to explain about the "monkey" comment. I also mentioned the problem Richard had with me, and I capped it all off with the toothbrush incident. As he absorbed the words I was saying, I could see the redness in his face, his veins were pulsating. He was getting pissed.

My victim was now leaning against a table, being attended to

132 while trying to balance himself on his shaky legs. The sergeant looked around and said, "Right! Uncuff him immediately. He is not being charged." He continued to bark at Richard, "If you dare to fire this man, I will do everything in my power to assist him with his wrongful dismissal lawsuit. Do I make myself clear on that?"

I was so proud of our police department. The cops understood me and stood by my side during this darkest hour. I will be indebted to my new friend, the sergeant, for life. I smiled as I watched him storm out of the sandwich shop, huffing and puffing his anger along the way. He was a cool dude, for a cop.

Everything after that day went from bad to worse. I didn't get fired, but I did get all of the crummy jobs. And, by the way, I didn't get the promotion when the Reynoldsburg store opened.

I put up with the crappy work for a couple of months before having enough of it. I was better off returning to the hustle. Losing myself and who I was to this type of demeaning employment was not worth the chicken scratch of a salary. It was a glorious day when I told them I was done. I left without having concrete plans for tomorrow. No worries; tomorrow will be dealt with tomorrow. For today, I will bask in my newfound freedom. Well, tomorrow did come and with a bang. That was the day that Regina told me she was expecting. I immediately got back into the hustle. Once again, I was a provider, but so much for working on the right side of the law.

Those were the quickest nine months, ever. I was twenty-nine years old when my perfect angel entered into this world and my heart. We named her Tiffany. Her childhood was like any other normal kid whose father was a gangster. I protected her and her brother from harm just by my reputation alone.

After leaving the sandwich shop. I started hanging around with
my motorcycle buddies more and more. We had a deep-rooted
past together, and that counted for something. They even gave me
my center patch and officially changed my name to "Warfare,"
a nickname that was fitting. I was now a full member of Heavy
Metal and with that came unlimited access to all other bike clubs.

Like every other time in my life when things were going my
way, a bump in the road would derail my plans. This time it wasn't
an ordinary bump in the road, something I would get over in a day
or two. This was a sinkhole of mammoth proportions. I got stopped
by a rookie police officer who was obviously trying to make an
impression on his superiors. His big score of the day—me!

Instead of giving me a ticket, like most other cops would do,
this chump started asking me all kinds of questions. This was the
one time I wished I looked more white. To him, I was just a Latino
thug who probably had a rap sheet as long as his arm. He was right
about the rap sheet. I answered all his questions without really
telling him anything. The first rule of thumb: never volunteer
information. Stick to the facts and only the facts. I was playing
by my rules and speaking only when spoken to. I guess he figured
out who I was by the radio chatter I could hear in the distance. He
called in my I.D. and a warning came back informing him that
I was wanted for absconding parole, back when I first left New
York for Ohio. I hadn't given much thought to any warrants that
might be floating around for me. It completely slipped my mind.
I was giving it a lot of thought now. I was in a pickle and there
was no one else to blame but myself. Skipping out on one's parole
agreement was a crime and punishable by a one-way ticket back
into the slammer, the last place I wanted to be. After being arrested

and held without bail for two weeks, two New York detectives arrived to escort me back to my former home town, New York City.

Regina, like every time before, followed me. My wife, son, and daughter moved back in with my mother-in-law in New York. Not my proudest moment. Being back in New York meant that Regina and the kids would be able to come and visit me on a regular basis. It would be a lot less expensive compared to travelling back and forth from Ohio. Seeing Regina on visiting day was more difficult for me than the hard time I was doing, and believe me, the time was hard. But compared with others, I guess you could say I was lucky enough to know many important people on the inside. Sing Sing was now my home. It wasn't where I wanted to be. How can this crap be happening to me now, when we just had a baby? This isn't what I wanted for Regina. I was sure that Regina didn't want this either.

My first day in the joint was an eye-opener. I couldn't believe how large La Familia had become. These guys were a major force to reckon with if you weren't a part of their family. As soon as I arrived into my wing, I recognized some friendly faces from the old days in Riker's Island and Elmira. We reminisced about the hellhole Riker's Island was (and still is apparently), and how we use to play ball at Elmira. I knew why they called themselves La Familia, and right now I was glad to be in their fold.

Not everything in prison makes sense. For example, my sister Iris had a baby named Emanuel ("God is with us"). We called him Mannie. When she would visit me, she would bring little Mannie with her. One of the guys pulled me aside and offered a piece of advice that at the time I didn't quite understand. He suggested that instead of playing with the baby and becoming too attached to him, I would be better off if I kept my distance. I asked him to explain. He suggested that by being too attached to the child, I would let my guard down. How can people keep their eyes focused on their surroundings while loving on a baby? I understood. There were a lot of enemies around, and all it would take is a moment of time for one of them to pounce. If my attention was diverted towards my nephew, I would be too slow to react, a dangerous thing to do. Again, I got his point. I knew our enemies were always watching us like birds of prey waiting for their next meal, their next kill. If I continued playing with the child, my time here would be harder, if not fatal. I had a real hard time wrapping my head around the concept of how my interaction with my nephew could possibly make a difference. Surely even my enemies understood the bond of family, loved ones from the outside. I couldn't stop thinking about Mannie. I was obsessed with the conflict. Do I ignore the child and regret missing those important times together? Do I risk being killed for what is really important to me: my family, my wife, my kids, and yes, my sisters and nephews too. Was I a gangster or a fool? I slept with one eye opened every night, just in case.

My Uncle Victor came to visit me, as he usually did when I was incarcerated. He would start off with the nice chitchat about my health, my family, and my needs. Then he would suddenly switch the conversation to God and the error of my ways. I politely listened while thinking to myself, "Here we go again."

When Uncle Victor left, he would add some cash to my prison account so I could have some spending money on the inside. He knew what it was like to be in here. My Aunt Zoriadia used to comment on how much I was becoming like Victor. Her words were so true. Every prison I entered had hallways graced by the presence of my Uncle Victor. While Victor preached at me, my mind wandered to Aunt Zoriadia. On the outside, I looked like I was listening, but on the inside, I was splitting a gut, laughing.

I spent the following months playing baseball and working out. If I wasn't hitting home runs or eating, I was lifting weights, doing pushups, and keeping my body in shape. It was beginning to show. The pounds fell off quickly and the muscle firmed up nicely.

Eventually, the time for my first parole hearing arrived. I could tell that most of the interviewers wanted to keep me there, thinking I was better off behind bars than on the streets. My wife wanted her man back home and spent all of her spare time speaking with people we knew in Ohio and asking them to write letters of reference. She showed up at my hearing with a stack of testimonials including some letters from companies in Ohio and New York City that guaranteed me employment upon my release. As they were read, I could feel myself getting all misty eyed. Maybe it was a combination of the letters, my wife's love and devotion, and the glossy look in my eyes that softened the hearts of the parole board. I no longer looked like a hardened criminal. Instead, I looked like a dad who missed his family and wanted to go home. I was granted parole.

I served a short prison run of eight months before finding myself on the streets once again, a free man. My debt to society was now paid in full. I immediately accepted one of the job offers promised to me. I began working full-time at a bakery in the heart of Manhattan. This was a first for me. I knew nothing about raising dough or baking cookies. I was glad to be there, learning a new trade. Once again, I would try to focus on the right side of the line

I would earn enough money to return my family to where I called home. I wanted to go back to Ohio where my kids could be raised and live a normal life. The problem was that the dark side kept calling my name.

After connecting with my brothers Croc and Cheddar and the others, I started feeling like I had never left the projects. Nothing there had changed, except for the crackheads that now appeared everywhere. I really missed Ohio, but it didn't take long before I started thinking about setting up shop right here in Brooklyn. All I needed was a little cash to get me going. My job was paying the bills, sort of, so it was just a matter of tightening up the belt, creating a budget, and soon enough we would be back on top once again. It would take the loving embrace of my wife to slap me back into the ugly reality of the Brooklyn streets.

One evening, while I passionately embraced my wife, I suddenly saw things clearly. There were too many people here that I had hurt. There was too much bad blood, and my staying here was just an invitation for something terrible to happen. My staying here was just making things easier for my enemies. The smart thing to do would be to run to Ohio as quickly as I could. That became my focus, my goal. As I said earlier, the problem was that the dark side kept calling my name.

Romans 12:19

Beloved, never avenge yourselves, but leave it to the wrath of God, for it is written, Vengeance is mine, I will repay, says the Lord.

Chapter 13: The Hit

Trying to make enough money to meet my needs was not that complicated. Sometimes you had to spend money in order to make money. As long as you invested correctly, profits were there for the making. An opportunity came up for an easy score. Buck, Pe Pe, Croc, and I would invest in the rental of a truck and use it to transport some weed from Kingsborough to Ohio where the customers were hungry for decent pot.

We ended up with 12 pounds of pot being fronted to us, which would translate into healthy profits, as long as nothing stupid happened along the way. As we finished loading the weed into the back of the truck, I had to ask myself if there was a better way to stack it. The bundles were stacked haphazardly on top of the other items within the truck (boxes, spare tire, tools, etc.). The stash was sitting there in plain view.

Before I could say or do anything, I saw two cops come walking down the street, right next to the truck. One cop started asking me a bunch of questions while the other one grabbed Croc and spun him around for a private chitchat of their own. I knew we were busted. My only thought was to do what I do best: hustle—all the way to the end. I could see Croc in the distance. He looked like he was smiling. I never saw him look so confident. It was as if he were saying, "Don't worry. Stay cool."

I worried and attempted to stay cool. *What the hell was Croc smiling at*? I pondered while trying to answer all the questions being thrown at me.

I never once gave up my hustle. I couldn't understand why this cop didn't notice the weed, stacked right there behind me. Then I saw his eyes staring at the back of the truck. *That's it. I'm going away for a long time*, I contemplated. I was waiting for the cop to start reading me my rights when all of a sudden the other cop came around to where we were standing. The cop that held me looked at Croc and said, "Why isn't the weed stacked on the bottom, out of sight? Are you trying to get yourself busted?"

With that, the two cops started laughing hysterically as they continued their way down the street. I was standing there, jaw dropped. I asked Croc, "What was that all about?"

Croc replied, "Whose weed do you think it is anyways?"

I was never formally introduced to those two cops (our partners), but I did see them occasionally around town. Rumor has it that they made so much money selling weed that they took an early retirement and are living somewhere in Florida, deep sea fishing. I said it before and I'll say it again, as long as you stick to selling weed and stay under the radar, the cops will leave you alone. It's the heroin and crack dealers they want to eradicate.

After rearranging the stacks so they were on the bottom with the rest of the junk on top, we hit the road. We arrived in Ohio 12 hours later.

Just before we left, Cheddar warned me, "I don't think those Ohio folks are going to give you a chance to make it there. You're not one of them. Those crazy white folks will kill you. You belong here with us. We're your people, not them."

I strongly believed that people were people, regardless of race.

Racism runs rampant in all races. They all have their good people and their bad. I just seem to react to the bad more than I do the good. I appreciated Cheddar's concern, but I knew he was wrong. If I could deliver high-grade weed to the people of Ohio, I would be revered, not victimized. I was right. I was soon heading back to New York on a weekly basis to meet the demand. Ohio was going through a pot dry spell which was good for my business.

I am a believer of sharing the wealth, and so it made sense to partner up with some of the local biker clubs, just to help us get our product out there more efficiently. These bikers had long-reaching arms that stretched out into every fiber of Ohio's population. During this era, if you were in Ohio and smoking weed, it was my weed you were getting high on. My reputation soon grew to where I was greeted as a friend in most places I visited. Every time I entered a club, I would buy a round of drinks for the house, regardless of how many there were. If you didn't like me, and you were in the club when I arrived, you got a free drink on me. That gesture went a long way to help keep the peace.

One day I was called to meet with the Heavy Metal's president and vice president. I accepted. They thanked me for coming and proceeded with a business proposition. They wanted to know if I was interested in becoming the club's enforcer. They described the responsibilities and highlighted the compensation and benefits. They gave examples of the work that I would have to do and asked me if I thought I was up to the task. Obviously, they didn't know me as well as they thought they did. There was nothing in the job description that worried me. I had done it all before, many times. I needed to show them that I was for real and a lot tougher than they gave me credit for. I took out by .38 revolver and removed all but three bullets. After spilling the cylinder, I placed the gun up to my head while keeping eye contact with the president. His eyes opened wider and a single bead of sweat ran down his nose. I squeezed the trigger. Click! Nobody moved. Nobody spoke. I then reloaded and holstered my piece. While continuing my stare I said, "I don't appreciate foolish questions, and I hate being toyed with. My game is for keeps. Am I clear on that?"

After the longest silence, the president broke out into nervous laughter, reaching for my hand. He understood as did everyone else there. I had their attention. I had their respect. Being their enforcer opened plenty of doors for me. I now had friends everywhere, and the experience I gained was priceless.

My pot business was still going strong with Buck and Pe Pe overseeing the daily operation. However, my responsibilities as enforcer were starting to get in the way. Being on call for Heavy Metal was eating up more and more of my time. This was no way to run a business. Something had to change and soon. Then opportunity came knocking at my door. The national president of the Nasty Boys came to me with a proposition. They wanted to open a chapter in Columbus and wanted to know if I was interested in an executive position. I told him that I would have to get back to him because I didn't want to burn any bridges with Heavy Metal. After speaking with my Heavy Metal advisor, I was told that I could go with the Nasty Boys and still retain the right to wear my Heavy Metal front colors. I would always be welcomed into their nest. I would always be considered a brother, for life. They added "Go in peace."

I began to pull in as many guys as I knew into my new Nasty Boys' chapter. If I knew you and you drove a motorcycle and weren already part of a gang, you were recruited. I even picked up some ex-Bloods and ex-Crips. This gang was growing faster than anyone imagined. The growing pains were felt at every level. There was so much to oversee but not enough eyes to keep watch. We had to pool our resources with other local gangs in order to stay on top of things. One of my guys, Fly, was also a leader with the South Side Crips. He came to me with a problem he was experiencing with an out-of-town gangster who was trying to move into occupied territory. Something needed to be done quickly before it got out of hand. We had a meeting to discuss the problem and to come up with a mutually satisfying solution. I did the only thing someone in my position could do: I called for a sit down, a meeting between all parties involved.

The park was overshadowed by the darkness of the night. There were thugs everywhere: some were mine and others were theirs. Upon our arrival, civilians quickly and quietly made their way to the nearest exit. Machine guns, shot guns, and pistols were everywhere. It was either the safest place or the most dangerous place to be, and I was right in the middle of it. Representatives from each side spoke their piece. I focused on what was being said while guns were pointed in my direction.

I must say, I was rather confused about the out-of-towners' request. They were asking for a spot in town to set up shop selling crack. Since our interest was primarily in the marijuana business, I couldn't see where the problem was. I really didn't care if they sold crack or not. If anything, I would prefer that they sell crack instead of my guys' selling it. Crack, like heroin, is a risky business. Pot is easy. Many like smoking weed. It doesn't destroy you as a person, it doesn't ruin your life, and it doesn't bring the wrath of the law down on top of you.

When I told them that I didn't have a problem with their request, they informed me that there was a conflict with my crack business. "What crack business?" I snapped back. This was when I found out that a few of my boys had actually started selling crack on their own, under the protection of my gang's affiliation. I was pissed! I told these guys to go with my blessings, and they could do as they requested as long as we got a piece of it. They agreed. I gained their respect for that.

Our combined forces did mean that we were now not only making more money, but it also meant that we were now a part of a crack-selling gangster ring, something I never wanted to do. It didn't take me too long to see that crack dealing was not going to work for us. I needed to separate the Nasty Boys from that line of business, and I needed to do it now. Pe Pe thought that the FBI was on to him, and that made all of us nervous. His job was to work with the south side boys and keep everyone out of trouble. We were now above the radar, not a comfortable place to be. I called for another meeting and made sure those who put us in this position attended. I needed to put things straight. These instigators didn't want to give up their lucrative crack business, so instead of speaking with words, my bodyguards and I started speaking in the enforcer language using baseball bats as our interpreter. When the bloody meeting was adjourned, the Nasty Boys of Columbus was a crack-free organization. Those in other gangs selling crack could keep their money — we were not interested.

I had to demote Pe Pe for the way he handled the situation. I was angry with him for not banging heads together when this first came up. It seemed as if only Buck and I were the ones making the tough decisions. It was exhausting.

Now that the crack thing was resolved and we were back under the radar, it was time to refocus on expansion. I had my eyes set on the east side of Columbus. There was a lot of opportunity there, ripe for the picking. Our first objective would be to set up shop in the projects called Oozie Alley. After finding an apartment there and negotiating with the local security guards, we were ready to open up for business. It was that easy. Of course, when you think that everything is going just fine, a wrench is thrown into the works, undoing all of your hard work. Everything fell apart the day one of my boys decided to kill one of the local gang members. All hell broke loose. The shooter was found hiding in Chicago and received 25 years to life for first degree murder. As a consequence, the first contract was taken out on me. Someone wanted me dead. Someone was setting me up.

I just turned thirty-three years old when Regina delivered our baby girl, my little angel, Crystal. This birth was a difficult one. My daughter just didn't want to come out. Regina was in great pain, and she could tell by the look on my face that I was experiencing each and every one of her torturous contractions. We were sharing the hurt, as one. When I saw Crystal's head start to show and then disappear back in again, I went into a panic mode. I opened the door to the corridor and dragged every person walking by into the room to help: doctors, nurses, custodians—I didn't care. My baby was in trouble, and I wanted help now!

Finally, the doctor arrived and I could tell by the serious look on her face that this was not going to be easy. She ordered the room to be cleared, including me. I wouldn't go. They actually had to manhandle me out of the delivery room. When my bodyguards, who were posted outside the delivery room, saw me being pushed and shoved by nurses, they immediately went into a protective mode. I had to shout at them, "No, no. It's okay. They're just kicking me out of the room so they can do what they need to do in there." My boys stood down. It was actually kind of funny when you think about it.

When my bodyguards and I reached the waiting room, the hospital police were there waiting. They were there just to make sure that there was no more chaos. Together, we all waited for word on Regina and Crystal. Picture this scene: a labor and delivery waiting room with a few fathers waiting for their babies to arrive. By the entrance there were four hospital cops and next to them were four mean-looking, aggravated, and nervous gangsters. Nobody wanted to be the first to speak. Finally, the doctor made her way over to where I was standing. I was waiting for her to tell me if Crystal was stillborn or not. I expected nothing else. I almost lost it. I felt like I was going to pass out under the stress of the moment. As the doctor took my hand into hers, I felt my heart push up into my throat. I couldn't breathe. She reassured me, "It's okay. It's okay. Do you need a sedative?"

I said, "No. Just tell me how the baby and Regina are."

"Mother and baby were fine."

Everybody smiled, including the cops and those other nervous fathers-to-be.

Now that Crystal was part of my life and that nasty crack business was behind us, it was time to party. For the next few months, life would continue along a predictable path. There were some issues that needed to be resolved, but like before, meetings were called, and conflicts were put to bed. I guess the decision for

peace never reached the guys who picked up the contract on me.
As far as they were concerned, I was a paycheck they had not yet
cashed. About three months after the birth of my daughter, their
payday opportunity would arrive.

I was partying with my Heavy Metal brothers while waiting
for the Imperial Bikers from New York to show up. These were
my boys from Brooklyn. It was going to be a great evening. There
was a family friend with us. When she wanted to go back to her
place, I decided to escort her, just to make sure she got back okay.
My bodyguards wanted to tag along, but since I believed we were
in a time of peace, I asked them to stay so they could greet our
Brooklyn friends. I told my bodyguards that I would be right back,
so they stepped down as I left the scene.

As I left the Heavy Metal Club, I heard someone say in a low
voice, "That's him." Something told me that I was in trouble. I
scanned my surroundings, trying to find a quick way to escape. I
had a real bad feeling that something awful was about to happen.
Within a moment, the first shot rang out. I was hit one millimeter
over my left eye. As my head was slammed backwards, an intense
pain shot throughout my entire body. If it had hit any lower, it
would have been a fatal wound. Everything else seemed to switch
into slow motion.

The weapon used was an assassin's .22, a very effective close
range gun. This was the weapon of choice by the New York mafia.
That was where the phrase was coined, "two in the back of the
head." After being hit in the head, my body slammed backwards
into a parked car. I was still able to focus on my survival. The only
thing I could think of was getting to my van where I had a stash of
guns waiting. I rolled off the car and started running.

This want-a-be hit man continued firing, unloading his entire clip, and slamming me against parked cars with each hit. His bullets found me five times. The first round got me in the head. My left arm received two shots, snapping my ulna bone along the way. A single shot went through my hand, and the last shot went into my left hip.

I was able to make it back to the clubhouse where my evening started. Nobody had heard the shots because of the loud music being played. I came crashing through the front door, landing on the floor, dying. I was rushed to Ohio State University Hospital where, needless to say, I survived. I woke up the next day with two detectives standing over me, wanting to know who I thought would do this to me. All I told them was Regina's name and phone number before returning to my drug-induced sleep.

When Regina received the call informing her that I had been shot, she initially thought it was a cruel, stupid joke. All Regina could think of was how I always said, "We never deal with crackheads. Those are the crazy ones who would kill you for a fix."

Wasn't selling weed supposed to be safe? The reality of what had happened was starting to set in. When Regina finally arrived at the hospital, the detectives got to her first with their 101 questions.

During the next two days, I remained in a coma. People came to visit me, but all they got to see was nothing more than a body connected to dozens of tubes and monitors. Medical staff came and went. Each time they entered my room, they had to deal with my bodyguards and the local authorities. The nursing staff argued that since guns were not permitted on the premises, all of this security wasn't necessary; nonetheless, my boys stood their ground. They would protect what was left of me, with brute force if needed.

Little did the nurses know that there were already many guns in the room, including one beneath my pillow. The police just sat back and allowed my boys to do their thing. The cops knew we were on top of things, and because the police didn't know who or what they were looking for, they sat back and watched my boys with hopes that we would do the detective work for them.

While the nurses were saying I was safe in their care, another attempt was being made on my life. This time it got no farther than the hospital's parking lot. The cops wouldn't get credit for this one, but instead it went to a Louisville slugger. He recognized two suspicious characters approaching the hospital and took them out immediately. They were armed and looking for me so they could finish the job. What was left of them was hauled away by the cops.

We had our boys everywhere. Heavy Metal's national president now gave strict orders: no one other than medical staff or family were permitted anywhere near the room. He knew what my blood family looked like, so as someone approached the door, he would look at him or her. Then a slight nod or tilt of his head this or that way would determine if that person would be permitted entry or not. His decision was final. No questions asked.

While all this was going on at the hospital, some of my boys went hunting for the shooters. They were eventually spotted and followed to their homes. I am not sure what happened to them, but I can say this: one moment they were there, and the next moment they were gone.

Once word got out about the attempts on my life, people started getting nervous about being implicated in the hits. The very next week someone wearing a mask entered the Heavy Metal clubhouse and started shooting at anything that moved. In total, one person was killed while three were seriously injured. Things in Columbus were starting to get out of hand. Everyone was going crazy. When I finally got out of the hospital, the motorcade that escorted me home was over the top. Talk about bringing attention to yourself. The first thing I did was to organize a sit down with the people I knew wanted me dead. I knew they were against me because I refused to sell crack, and they would never get over it. They wanted my apartments, and they wanted me out. I came up with a plan and was able to smooth things over, and with that, I handed my business over to my crew. It was now their problem. Good luck with that! I didn't want the gangster life anymore. If I didn't get out now, it would only be a matter of time before I made the leap over the line into the realm of murder. I wasn't ready to take a life. I could beat up someone, but at least I knew that person would continue to breathe when I was done. Killing someone was a whole new game I didn't want to play. Crack was now everywhere, and if you weren't a part of it, you were missing out on some serious cash. However, I still had my scruples. Crack and I would never play well together.

Genesis 9:6

Who so sheddeth man's blood, by man shall his blood be shed: for in the image of God made he man.

Chapter 14: A State Champion

Everybody has his or her limit. You can only take so much before reaching a breaking point. My breaking point was being shot and almost killed. I loved my wife and kids too much to simply die before walking my daughters down the aisle or giving my son fatherly advice. This gangster life was killing me, literally. I was at a crossroads, so my destiny was riding on which direction I would decide to go. Go the right way and I just might have a chance; my family might just have a chance. Go the wrong way and my destiny would be locked in like a sealed casket.

Getting out of the gangster business was difficult. There was nothing else I could do that would bring in such a lucrative income. But then again, what good is money to me when I am six feet under?

Some of my friends from the Zanesville Flames Motorcycle Club were working at a local factory. If it was good enough for them, it was good enough for me. I started working at the factory making a decent wage while trying to cut down on my gangster habits. Just because I was working a regular nine-to-five job didn't mean I was all sweet and innocent. I continued to sell small amounts of pot, just to bring in a little extra cash. It helped. As far as being an enforcer or negotiator, those days were behind me.

I found myself drinking more and more during those days. I knew if I didn't find a new focus, and soon, I could possibly start

152 having an affair with the bottle. Being shot in the head rewired my brain somehow. I was thinking differently and speaking differently. I was also driven like never before.

My new goal was to sign up at the Rick Moore Academy to learn the skill of martial arts. My kids and I would share in this experience and that helped fuel the fire that was my determination to succeed. I needed to be the best. Something took over inside of me. Every lesson was like a breath of fresh air. The more I inhaled, the stronger I became. However, my injuries and the scars they left were a hindrance. I still spoke with a slight slur and had trouble processing complete sentences. When people spoke to me, I would have trouble understanding what they were trying to say. Yes, I heard the words, but I just couldn't put them together in my mind. These would be my emotional scars of a former life, the ugly life of a gangster.

When Tiffany, Crystal, and Louis Junior were old enough, I enrolled them into a martial arts program. They would follow their daddy's footsteps. My kids would be able to defend themselves, if needed. The self-defense classes were especially important for Louis Junior because he was born smaller than normal. As his body developed, his legs and arms tightened up on him. His heart was giving him trouble as well. If it weren't for the constant stretching during his martial arts classes, he would most likely have grown up with some severe physical handicaps.

For Tiffany, I joked about her going on dates and using her self-defense skills to stop a boy from going too far. Tiffany took to the martial arts training really well. She was a natural, eventually winning state and national championships.

One time when we were sparing, she hit me with a roundhouse

kick, landing it with full force on my upper lip. I never saw it 153
coming. I was never more proud of her as I was when I stood there holding onto my bloody lip. I wear the scar like a badge of honor.

My only purpose—other than being a great father and husband—was to study the martial arts. I was drawn towards the discipline of controlling that anger that boiled deep within. I was learning how to tame the beast. I started absorbing every martial arts book I could get my hands on. Master Moore recognized the spark in my eye and the fire in my stance. He gave me a book titled *Musashi* and told me to study it. This book was about the life of a great sword man and the trials and tribulations he endured while pursuing his dream. By the time I finished the book, I saw a vision of what I was supposed to do with my life. It was as clear as glass to me. I immediately quit my job at the factory and told Master Moore that I wanted to work for him at the academy. He thought I was out of my mind, delirious from drinking too much or maybe just crazy from my gunshot head injury. Master Moore barked, "Why didn't you talk with me before quitting your job?" I didn't have a good answer. He continued, "Do you know anything about running a karate school?"

Of course, I had to reply with "No."

He called Regina and told her what I had done. The two of them then ganged up on me trying to convince me that I was not thinking straight. They thought I was putting the cart before the horse. I didn't understand their resistance. Why couldn't they see my vision as clearly as I did?

I started to understand Master Moore's hesitation once he sat me down and explained a few things to me. Obviously, having a beginner's yellow belt didn't give me the authority I needed to command the respect of the students. Black belts only need apply! Adding to my lack of experience was the fact that he didn't have any openings at the school. Then I slowly started to realize that maybe this time I did indeed jump a little too fast. Master Moore suggested that I get a job, continue training, and allow the future to unfold until the time was right. Wise words!

Regina and I would continue this conversation at home. We argued for some time, or should I say, she yelled and I listened? Regina was trying her best to talk me out of my vision even though she didn't really grasp what it was. I understood what Master Moore was saying about taking baby steps. I could understand why he didn't see things as I did. Nevertheless, my wife should understand. I had a hard time accepting the idea that she didn't see things as I did. I continued to try to explain my dream to her while she continued to tell me I was wrong. It was a long day and even longer night.

I never wanted something so bad before. I knew if I worked at the academy I could continue to learn the business of running a school and growing as a martial artist at the same time. The dream was so tangible that I could taste it. I went back to speak with Master Moore the next morning. I wasn't going to give up that easily. Master Moore and I talked some more about my situation. I even played my sympathy card by telling him that it was a great way for me to help my son Louis to deal with his weak legs and heart. The master pondered as I continued showing him what was within my heart. Now he was listening to me instead of arguing. I even had a game plan put together. As I started explaining every detail, the master looked closely at me, trying to decide if I was drunk or if there actually was something to my plan. I laid out

the details of a commission structure and suggested that he give
me a week to prove my point. I can sell ice to Eskimos, so selling academy membership plans would be easy for me. The more memberships I sold would mean more money for the academy, and me. My people skills were well-known and as far as selling goes, I guess I did a good job in convincing Master Moore. He was sold. He liked the idea of selling more memberships and loved my determination. I was now employed at the academy, earning a salary based on commission. The more I sold, the more I earned. I was in control of my destiny and my dream.

The academy had various plans you could sign up for. Plan "A" was a basic $150 introductory program. Plan "B" cost $250 and covered many more classes. Plan "C" was a full year subscription, paid in advance. I would focus on selling Plan "C" as that gave me the largest commission.

Every week I was making good money, much more compared to the factory work I recently walked away from. Because my weekly earnings were growing, it meant Master Moore's school was also growing. Nearly everyone who entered the building to seek information was sold a plan. I even helped create a new look for "Buddy Night." Kids could come in and bring a friend. They would be taught some basic self-defense moves followed by playing some games. We would even have a movie night for the kids along with a weekend sleepover. It was all coming together. My spirit was on fire, and the master was proud of me. He learned to listen to my dreams.

People who quit before their contracts were fulfilled had a negative effect on my income. It was known as the leaky bucket syndrome. The only way to make sure customers, especially the kids, stay was to make the classes fun. We incorporated a fun atmosphere into our routine, and in the long run, it paid off. I was signing clients left and right. Classes were at or near capacity. The leaky bucket syndrome was becoming more and more rare, just the way I liked it.

There is a certain point when one knows that what he or she is doing is appreciated by the boss. My magical moment of accomplishment came when Master Moore sent me on a business trip to California. It was a weeklong martial arts seminar and my job was to represent the Rick Moore Academy. It was one of my proudest moments. Master Moore was glowing with pride as well. He would tell his colleagues all about me and my dream. He would laugh saying, "I've created a monster," in reference to how I absorbed everything that was thrown at me. I was a sponge with no limit. My green belt came easy to me. I continued training, learning, and advancing.

Master Moore once said he only hired black belts. He ate his words when he allowed me to start teaching karate classes while I was still a green belt. He knew where I was going and how quickly I was going to get there. I didn't slow down. All I saw was the path ahead of me. There was no time to think about anything else. I focused my attention on making Master Moore's school bigger and better. Because Master Moore felt compelled to help other schools grow, he would send me to other karate schools to come up with ideas for their growth. His growth was rewarding, so he felt obligated to offer advice to smaller schools with administrative management problems. Most of the time my advice would land upon deaf ears; perhaps my green belt status held the other masters back from listening to what I had to say. Sometimes they were so open to my words, but at other times it was like talking to a wall.

I knew when I returned from studying a school's methods, Master Moore would ask me, "How can we make that school you last visited a better one?" The question was always the same. To be more efficient, I started preparing a detailed report on each facility I visited. As soon as Master Moore asked that same old question, I would hand him my report and wait patiently for his reply. Since these other facilities weren't listening to what I had to say directly, Master Moore would take my report, call the schools, and tell them that they needed to do this or that, all based the recommendations within my report. Once they took the advice and gained from it, Master Moore would look them in the eye and tell them that they had Louie to thank for their success. Imagine that, a green belt suggesting how other masters should run their schools. Those were extraordinary moments for me and Master Moore.

Whenever masters visited our academy, I rolled out the red carpet and treated them like royalty. I looked at them with reverence and treated them as such. My reputation quickly spread to all the other schools. Everybody knew who Louie was. I was becoming known as the "business-minded green belt." I liked it a lot better than my biker-club name, "Warfare." Eventually, I started receiving offers from many other karate disciplines. They were offering me and my family free crash courses in their own unique systems, including kung fu, shotokan, tae kwan do, judo, kick boxing, and even Okinawan karate (also known as Matsubayashi). Being the information sponge I was, I absorbed everything they had to offer.

If you want to learn what persistence means, look at my son Louis. Remember, he was training while dealing with his physical limitations. For the first two years of tournaments, he lost every

158 single bout. He had zero wins. Most people would have given up but not my son. He continued boldly and without fear. His strength was his determination. Master Moore took Louis under his wing and treated him like family. Louis actually called Master Moore "grandpa." Whenever Louis was defeated at a competition, he would turn to Master Moore and ask, "Grandpa, when is the next tournament?" It would bring tears to my eyes. To me, his determination was a victory worth celebrating, and we did. After Louis' twenty-five consecutive losses, he won the biggest tournament of his career. He beat forty-five competitors in his ring and walked away with his division's state grand championship. If that wasn't enough, my daughter Tiffany and I also took our division titles on the same day. There would be three trophies on the Lugo mantle that night. Regina never doubted my dreams again.

A long time ago, something told me to quit my job at the factory to chase a dream that didn't make sense to anyone, especially to me. My wife and I argued that night, and Master Moore told me I wasn't ready. But something deep inside, in a place I never knew even existed, was commanding that I blindly follow. I did. Look at me today, with a trophy in hand, watching my kids follow in my footsteps and excel. Maybe there is a God!

Gen 37:19

Here comes that dreamer!' they said to each other.

Chapter 15: The Crossroads

For a while life seemed to be going my way. I was successful at work and at play. My family was benefiting from the martial arts classes, and Regina was never more proud of me. I did enjoy my occasional downtime with my friends in the motorcycle clubs. They respected what I was doing with my life and the new man I had become. I respected them for their understanding. I was all karate. Nothing else entered my mind. It was a matter of doing what I knew and trying to learn what I didn't know. I tried to gain knowledge from any source I could find, especially from Master Moore.

One day Master Moore was telling me how he faces his opponents. He said that once he is in the ring, he faces his competitors one at a time saying, "I'll beat you!" He would continue this until he addressed every single competitor. I realized he was trying to weaken his opponents with head games. I knew I wanted to try this new technique. I was sure it would work for me.

My time came to put this new approach to the test. I entered the ring and saw my competitors waiting for me. I decided to add a little flare to the technique. I boldly stood there pointing a finger at each one while saying loudly, "I'll beat you!"

The fights started and I did quickly beat each one of them. The plan was simple. Make my opponent angry by pointing and yelling before the fight. When he/she loses his/her focus and rushes at you,

160   a quick step backwards, followed with a quick side kick would put me on the offense, a better place to be. I thought to myself how amazing Master Moore was and couldn't wait to learn some more of his little secrets. My motto was becoming "see one, do one, and teach one." I was now ready for the next level.

It wasn't until the competition was over that Master Moore explained to me that when he said, "I'll beat you," he was actually thinking the words while looking them in the face. Nothing audible ever passed his lips while in the ring. Yelling at your competitor was not considered proper protocol. To his foe, he wasn't saying the words, just thinking them. To his opponents, he was simply acknowledging them while within his own mind he was telling himself what he was about to do. Here I was pointing my stupid finger at these guys while barking like a mad man. I now realized I had so much more to learn. I was starting to feel a little inadequate within the martial arts' world.

There were times when I would be defeated; those days were hard for someone like me. I remember losing one fight in Cincinnati and after it was over, I was trying to analyze where went wrong. It was obvious to those around me that I was coming down hard on myself. Suddenly a man came out of nowhere and started speaking to me in a calming voice. He reassured me that being defeated was part of the journey to greatness. I looked up at him and immediately sensed a calming effect overtaking my body and mind. As quickly as he appeared, he vanished. With my newly boosted ego, I started to search for this man. Then I saw him on the other side of the hall surrounded by a large crowd. They were pestering him for his autograph. It was at that moment that I realized who he was. My mystery friend was the famous world champion Anthony Price. I was starstruck, impressed, and awed.

Anthony Price was the kind of man who would go out of his way to help others, especially if that person was just starting out in martial arts. He had a large fan base and wasn't too shy to give back whenever the opportunity arose. It became a part of his legacy, so I glowed knowing I was one of the lucky ones to have received a gift of his kindness and compassion. It was Anthony Price's influence on me that gave me that extra motivation to go on and win the Ohio State Championship for kata (forms), kumite (fighting), and weapons.

Now when I speak about winning a championship, I know there was no way I should have advanced to the finals. Because I still hung around with my motorcycle friends, I had a fondness for drinking, or should I say, I had a passion for it. Tournaments made me a little nervous so the day before a match, I would go out and party hard. The next day I would be in the ring, facing my foe, extremely hung over. At first, I just attributed it to my nerves, but as time passed, I started to recognize that the booze was beginning to overtake who I was. My priorities were shifting from my dream of running my own martial arts school to getting the day over as quickly as possible so I could return to my buddies at the club.

When Regina, my grounding rod, told me that I had a drinking problem, I told her that she didn't know what she was talking about. Yes, there was a problem; however, it took me a long time to realize that the problem was me and all the crap from my past. I was standing at a crossroad and it looked like I was making wrong decisions on which way I should go. Was my crossroad leading me to a dead end?

Yes, Regina and I wanted to open our own karate school. I had a couple of years of experience now working at the Rick Moore Academy. My family joined me on my journey, and now they were accomplished martial artists with trophies of their own. Within the martial arts community, I had a solid reputation, except for my drinking issue. It was one of those subjects that people just didn't bring up, that is, except for my wife. Regina was the only one who realized the cause of my weakness. She recognized the post traumatic stress syndrome I was living with each and every day—a result of being shot five times.

Master Moore was concerned about the obvious addiction I had with the bottle, but as long as I kept my promise to never drink while in school, he accepted who I was. If only he knew the real reason for my drinking. He knew I was a good martial artist and had the respect of others. He let me know that he was there for me, if I ever needed him. I appreciated that. I continued to grow as a man and as a martial artist.

Despite all the obstacles I created for myself, Regina and I went ahead with our plans to open our school. Johnstown, Ohio, would be our location, and we were both excited about what the future had in store for us. I was now a brand new, first degree black belt, and in some ways, not feeling qualified to run a school. On the other hand, my experience running Master Moore's school gave me the special training I needed to be a success with my own facility.

Getting my black belt was a dream come true. Being a brown belt for over three years, I was eager to get up to the next level. Whenever the black belt tests would come up, Master Moore would tell me, "Not yet. Be patient."

I wasn't very patient. I knew I was ready and couldn't understand why others thought I wasn't. During my years as a sergeant to the brown belts, I must have helped approximately thirty-five to forty-five brown belts receive their black belts. I knew I was ready, now.

Eventually my day of advancement came. It was time for me to test for my black belt. On that day, I would be the only one being tested. That was fine by me. It would be less confusing that way. I was focused and hungry for black. It took so long for that special day to arrive, and yet looking back, it all happened so fast. I clearly remember that day; it was just like any other, except for the last minute change in the schedule. When I arrived at work and found out that there was a brown and black belt workout added to the schedule, I was somewhat frustrated and confused. Usually I am made aware of these events but not this one. At first I didn't give it much thought, that is, until I noticed masters from out of state arriving. Something was up. Out of state masters never showed up unless something was going on; these were the big boys. Normally, once Master Moore invited these guys, I would be brought into the loop immediately so I could prepare for their red carpet treatment. This day was different. I had no notice, no opportunity to prepare. This sort of thing had happened before, although rarely, so I just rolled with it and helped out wherever I could.

After my two-and-a-half hour workout was finished, I suddenly realized what was going on. Everyone under the age of twenty-five was asked to leave the premises. I was given 15 minutes to prepare for my traditional black belt testing. I gave it my all. I gave blood, pain, and everything else I had to offer. The fatigue was overpowering, yet like the days when my Uncle Victor tried to beat me down, I remained on my feet facing the challenge with a hunger for more. Then without notice, the rumble was over. Everyone stood down, bowing towards me, and again towards the board of judges. There was peace and calm as each opponent approached me with congratulations. I was now a black belt. I was one of the few who made it to this level. I was disciplined and accomplished. I went to the bathroom to catch my breath, in solitude. As I peered into the mirror, I smiled at the black eye, which was the same color as my belt. It hurt so good. I inhaled slowly because my two broken ribs sent jolts of pain throughout my body. It hurt so good. As I reentered the hall and joined the others, I basked in the glow of what I had done. My dream was coming true. I didn't even think about drinking that night. It hurt so good.

I owed much of my success to my friend Master Mike Taylor. He was the one who taught me the importance of a proper kick. Learning front, side, wheel, axes, crescent, and roundhouse kicks all consumed hour upon hour, day upon day, weeks, months, and even years of training. Mike would watch my kicking style, instructing me to repeat it over and over until I got it right. When I finally got it down, Mike would beam with genuine happiness. When I messed up, he would push me harder. This was his secret. Later, when Master Mike passed away, a piece of me died with him, but my kicks remained intact.

Now that our Johnstown school was officially opened, it was time for me to put my black belt to use. I was teaching kids what I knew from my teaching and administrative experience at the Rick Moore Academy. I was now ready for the dream to be finally fulfilled.

A special day for Regina and me was the day we held our first testing for white belts advancing to yellow. Because of the way I treated all of the visiting masters at the Rick Moore Academy, they came to my school and returned the favor by treating me and my students with the highest level of respect. It was like watching the masters when they test a bunch of black belts. My students were being honored and my tearful eyes told them that something special was happening. Master Moore came up to me and told me how proud he was of all I had done. No one had ever said they were proud of me before. More tears flowed.

As time passed, my students were ready for their first tournament. We were off to Columbus with parents in tow. Everyone was nervous and a little afraid. These were country kids from the small town of Johnstown with a big city attitude. They used every trick I taught them; tricks that all of the masters taught me to help me win in the ring. My students took first and second place in sparring and first to third places in kata and weapons. These victories were not only encouraging for my students but also validating for me. I knew who I was and what I was doing. My dream was in the here and now. It was real.

Within two years, my school was training state champions. We were so well known that my students were invited to perform during the half-time show for the Columbus Quest, the world champion women's basketball team. Parents saw a positive change in their kids, including better grades and improved attitudes at home. My school was making a difference in our little community, so when people saw me or anyone from my family walking down the street, we were treated like family. Their warmth was inviting and infectious. Life was good, that is, until a forgotten speeding ticket suddenly surfaced.

There was a traffic warrant issued for my arrest. I received a ticket in Columbus some time earlier and had completely forgotten

166 about it. It's not as if I was that same gangster who would spit on the shoes of authority. I was now a law-abiding citizen, so when my day in court came up, I went with a determination to tell the truth and pay my dues, no matter how much that would be. I did have a little advance notice from a police officer who came to my school and told me about the warrant. He suggested that I go directly to Columbus and take care of the warrant. Even though I still got nervous around cops, police stations, and courthouses, I took his advice. When my lawyer explained to the judge that the Johnstown police officer never arrested me but instead suggested that I come to Columbus to resolve the warrant, the judge was dumbfounded. It was the last thing he expected to hear. Looking at me, he probably expected some sort of gangster set of lies. The cop should have arrested me since there was an actual warrant issued, but he didn't because Johnstown was a small town, and he knew I would do the right thing. The small town attitude was what prevented my arrest. The judge saw the truth for what is was and slammed down his gavel, killing the warrant. Case dismissed. Yes I live in Johnstown and was proud of it. The cop, my friend, who told me about the warrant did me a great favor. I was glad to be finally walking on the right side of the law.

Isaiah 48 : 15

I, even I, have spoken; yes, I have called him. I will bring him,
and he will succeed in his mission.

Chapter 16: God's Lesson

We named our school Johnstown Shorin Ryu Karate. For three years, our doors had been open to all who were seeking what we had to offer: exercise, discipline, and an outlet for pent-up anger and frustration. Can you believe it? I was a business owner for over three years and helping others become better people at the same time.

Because our new school was competing, we spent a lot of time traveling around Ohio. It really didn't matter what circuit we were in, we commanded the ring, taking home trophies by the busload. We were winning first to third place titles like we owned them. We did!

The reasons for a child to take self-defense classes vary like the weather. No two children are the same. Each kid has his or her own monsters to deal with, so what we taught them helped them to cope. It was the parents who looked at us as the last resort. Their kids could be experiencing disciplinary or physical hardships or issues such as Attention Deficit Disorder (ADD) or Attention Deficit Hyperactivity Disorder (ADHD). Sometimes the child was simply a loner or might be a victim of bullying at school. All of these can be devastating for the child and his or her parents. What we taught helped build up that missing self-confidence and sew the fabric of the family back into one cohesive unit. There was nothing more gratifying than to see parents interact with their child with love and adoration versus the coldness they displayed when they first showed up at my door. For me and Regina, it was emotionally rewarding.

We were so plugged into our community that it was common to see our students doing outreach programs: fixing leaky roofs, doing yard work for the elderly and the inflicted, or bringing a meal to someone who was in need. We even put on demonstrations at the Johnstown Home for the Elderly and at the public library. Whenever we arrived somewhere, people would gather. It was amazing. For someone with a past as colorful as mine, it was nice to be finally considered one of the good guys. I had 184 students, and I loved each and every one of them. I was making a decent living too.

Just when you think everything is going your way, something always happens to pull the rug out from beneath your feet. Uncle Victor would come by on occasion to check up on how things were going. Sometimes I would go to his place to brag about my students and their amazing achievements. Victor still had a lot of negativity in him and would often lecture me by saying things such as, "Everything you are doing means nothing in the long run." He would also say, "You think you are doing something great but in reality nothing has really changed."

I tried to explain to him that my accomplishments were no different from his. Then he would start lecturing me about God. He would argue, "Louie, everything I do is for the glory of God, to show His mercy and grace." He would add, "What you are doing only glorifies man." He would also say, "I've heard about all that you are doing in Johnstown and I think it's great, but if you are giving yourself the recognition, then there is no meaning behind it. It has no worth or value in this world."

I would walk away confused, and yes, maybe a little hurt and angry. Talk about bursting one's bubble. It was true. I was walking around proud of my accomplishments, and yes, the parents and community were giving me glory for what I was doing. I was trying to live a righteous life, the only way I knew how, without God. As a result, by living without God, I was deaf to what my uncle was trying to teach me. I didn't realize it at the time, but because of my hardened heart, the Devil was about to strike with a vengeance. His blow would be crippling to me and my family. He would hit me hard and knock me down for the count. God was still nowhere to be found within my world. Victor tried to warn me.

I would often ask students' parents to help with fundraising. One of my students parents decided to not turn in the money they collected. For them, keeping the cash was a mini-windfall, a temptation difficult to walk away from. I confronted them. The day after my confrontation with the embezzling parents, I was accused of fondling three of my female students, one of them being their daughter. These were girls who came to me with serious issues. The first one was experiencing drug addiction, the second one dressed and acted like a hooker, and the third one was involved with gangs. I knew where these troubled kids were coming from, so I had a complete understanding of who they were deep down inside. Their parents didn't know them like I did, so that was the beginning of the problem. When I addressed the fundraising issue, their guilt forced them to lash out at me the only way they knew how. They stuck their virtual dagger right into my heart and twisted it with intent to do as much harm as they could, taking the attention off of their thievery at the same time. It worked.

For a small town like Johnstown, these accusations spread through the community like a tornado leaving destruction along

170   its path. I tried to ignore the accusations, brushing them off as being ridiculous, and they were. Charges were filed and a plea deal was placed on the table for me to consider. I laughed it off. Why should I negotiate for something I didn't do? I wasn't a pervert. I was an instructor of the martial arts. Sure there is physical contact, the same for boys as for girls. When their head is tilted wrong or their foot is positioned incorrectly, it is common to take the foot or head and move it into the right position. There was nothing sexual about it. These points were ignored by the detectives' investigation of the allegations. The girls were interrogated in the living room of one of the families involved, not in a controlled environment like police headquarters. By legal standards, their statements were considered to be contaminated and non-admissible; nevertheless, the prosecution used them. During the trial, none of the girls could actually pinpoint a time and place when the alleged inappropriate touching happened. Their testimony was wrought with nervous inconsistencies.

All I wanted was to get back to my students and my family. I wanted to be the local community hero, not the resident pervert. The detective who took the stand to testify against me stated that because of her vast experience in these matters, she was convinced that I was guilty as charged. Vast experience, right! She attended two seminars on the science of sexual perversion and the behavior patterns of a sexual deviant over a two-year period, each one no more than an hour long. The 11 white jurors, those who saw me as a hardened criminal, were leaning in, hanging on to each and every lie that was being said about me. The one and only black female juror stood out like a sore thumb. Her opinion wouldn't make any difference.

When my wife took the stand to testify for me, the entire room got so quiet I could hear my heartbeat. Her words meant nothing. To my accusers, she was merely a wife standing up for her man. If anything, they were disappointed that Regina wasn't furious with me for doing what they said I had done. Regina knew me, so she knew I didn't do what they said I did. The trial was quick and efficient. Most of the time was spent listening to the accusers with little rebuttal from the defense. "Klan" justice was at play. In the nearby town of Mayberry, protests were being held in support of the defense. They knew it was all a lie. "Let him go! Let him go!" was chanted up and down the streets. The Johnstown folks joined in for moral support. The citizens of Mayberry and Johnstown were behind me all the way. The problem was that my trial was held in Newark, Ohio. To these folks, I was an unknown, a gangster, and a pervert.

Regardless of the character witnesses lining up to testify on my behalf, I was found guilty as charged. Only eight people were allowed to speak about my good qualities; the director of child services said some wonderful things about me. The judge had heard enough and exclaimed, "Case closed!" The Devil had won the day.

Regina, who was now pregnant with our fourth child, sat there stunned as the judge read the verdict. His glare never left my wife's eyes as he said, "Mr. Lugo, I sentence you to three consecutive, three year terms, one for each victim, in a state facility starting immediately." Regina passed out, landing on the floor. The entire courtroom gasped. Everyone from both sides was crying. The prosecution side cried because they never expected me to receive such a long sentence, and the defense side cried because I was

172 railroaded. I didn't cry. I was too stunned. I was furious. How could this be happening to me now? The local newspaper actually misquoted me. It printed my statement as, "The jury did a good job." In reality what I said was, "The jury did a good job at kissing the KKK's ass!" It seems as if they left out a few important words.

I was now once again a convicted felon. At 40 years old, I thought my criminal life was behind me. It just goes to show, the Devil never sleeps. As I was cuffed and removed from the courtroom, I glanced over at Master Moore who was standing there watching me. I could see his mouth form the words, "Nothing has changed."

I knew exactly what he meant. You see, Master Moore was raised in this town and being a black man, he knew all too well how the blinders of justice worked. He knew they would find me guilty before the trial actually started. As I was led down the hallway, I saw my good friend Fly in the distance. He was standing there watching me. Seeing him made all of the anger flush away. My shock was gone. I knew it was payback time, and Fly was going to see that justice was done, one way or another. I knew the people who had stolen the money from the fundraiser and started this ridiculous episode in my life were going to have a debt to pay, and Fly was going to be the collector. He formed a gentle smile. Newark wouldn't see the last of me.

Yes, there was anger brewing deep down inside me, an anger I had known all too well. Fly and some of the boys were there to offer me moral and physical support. The judge was not aware of the boys being there. Everyone from my former crew had traded in their leathers for three-piece suits. They had shaved and washed and tied back their hair. They were there for me, incognito. Th judge had a gut feeling that something was up. He knew my past and those I associated with. He believed that once a person becomes a gangster, he or she will always be a gangster. So much for his faith in the system of rehabilitation.

As I was being led out, I could hear the judge warning me and all in his courtroom, "If any harm should befall these brave and victimized families, Mr. Lugo will be held personally responsible. Do I make myself clear on that?"

My former associates were already hatching their plan. They would follow my accusers home and strike fast and hard. They ignored the judge's commands. I looked at Regina one last time. As our eyes met, she knew what was in my heart. She understood three things: she believed I was innocent; she believed in my dream, so she would see that the momentum at the school would continue, even with my being behind bars; and finally, she knew that she would have to speak with the guys on my behalf to stop the blood bath that they were planning. My lips whispered, "I love you."

Regina smiled, cried, and then she was gone, doors slamming shut behind me as I was led to a holding cell. My transportation was being arranged and soon I would be back in the darkness of the prison world, a place I had not wanted to see ever again. And yes, I screamed out loud for all ears to hear, "I didn't do it!"

Later on that day, Regina and I did speak through a bullet-proof glass partition. She told me that she was pregnant. My anger quickly faded, being replaced with my love for my wife and the unborn child within her. Revenge now left a nasty taste in my mouth, and I wanted no part of it. As we talked, in code, Regina confirmed my wishes that none of these families were to be harmed in any way. At first, I hungered for retaliation, but something inside of me changed. Now all I wanted was peace, not violence. I needed her to speak with the various gang leaders on my behalf. There was no time to waste. When the visit ended, I knew she would be entering a dangerous world. On the outside, I looked all brave and stoic, but on the inside I was a nervous wreck. I didn't get much sleep that night for fear of what might happen out there while I was in here, caged and helpless.

My former bodyguard stayed with Regina as she made her rounds to the various gang leaders pleading my wishes. They all knew her from the old days and showed her the respect that they would have shown me. By the time she was done, it was solidified: there would be no war of retribution. No blood would be spilled, and Regina was assured that if there was anything she needed, anything at all, all she had to do was ask. Now, it was up to the appeals process. Maybe the truth would finally be told, or should I say, maybe the truth would finally be heard and believed. The waiting game began.

I was escorted to the state prison reception in Orient, Ohio. Even though I had been incarcerated before, I'd never seen a place like this, where snitches ran wild, and the administrators were soft and mild-mannered. In the New York prison system, the warden and guards were hard core and mean. That was all there was to it. They could beat you down and then enjoy a nice lunch without giving you a second thought. Here, in this facility, everything was so foreign to me. I couldn't wait to leave. Deep down inside I knew that one of my accusers would step forward, tell the truth, and set me free.

One of the girls composed a letter and mailed it to the judge

telling him that I never did any of the things I was accused of. *175*
However, the letter was anonymous. There was no way of knowing
which child typed the confession. There were details in the letter
that only the girls or their parents would know about, so it did catch
the judge's attention. During all of this, one of the girls went to a
priest and confessed that I was innocent. When my lawyer found
out about this, he tried to get me released immediately. He failed.
When my lawyer found out about the letter to the judge, again
he thought I was going to be released. He was wrong. The judge
wanted to speak with each of the girls to determine who wrote
this letter. Then, and only then, would he entertain the notion of
reversing his decision. Finding and interviewing these three girls
was no easy task. All the while, I stayed in prison. While waiting
for the prosecutor and judge to sort out the lies, I settled in for the
long haul.

The prosecutor decided to go to one of the girl's school to pick
her up for questioning. When the judge heard about the prosecutor's
interrogation, he hit the roof, giving the prosecutor a piece of his
mind. "There are protocols for that sort of thing," he snapped to the
now very nervous prosecutor. The judge continued with his lecture,
"It is inappropriate for you to pick up this girl or any young lady
in that fashion." He closed with a stern warning to the lawyers on
both sides, "I will not stand for that sort of behavior." The message
was received loud and clear.

The girl denied writing the letter to the judge. She was
taken home, and as far as the next girl went, arrangements were
made for her and her parents to come down to the courthouse
for a conversation about the mysterious author. She also denied
composing the letter. It was clear now whom they were looking

for. It was girl number three. Finding her was challenging and time consuming. This was the girl who started the whole thing. We had proof of her lies during the trial, but we were not permitted to enter the evidence because of some legal formalities. When it was time for her to come in and answer some questions regarding that letter, she was nowhere to be found. Apparently her mother took her out of state. I would find out years later that the mother intimidated her by saying, "If you wrote that letter and tell them the truth, mommy will go to jail for a long long time."

After two weeks, the third, mentally-brainwashed child was returned home and immediately questioned about the letter. She denied being the author. Really!

It looked like my stay in the can would be a long one. I was pissed! People who saw me walking by would give me a wide berth. The anger was written all over my face, and I wasn't afraid to show it. I told my story to anyone willing to listen. It seemed to help me deal with the anger. Guys thought I was crazy, and they all had advice as to how to seek revenge. I wanted to fight so bad I could taste it, but I resisted the urge. The last thing I needed was to create trouble on the inside. I needed to keep my nose clean, at least for now.

After being there a week or two, the dorm sergeant returned from vacation. He recognized me from my school. When he heard my story, he called me to his office and sat me down for a one-on-one conversation. He reminded me that I had a lot of friends in here, and my time could be easy time. Apparently, many of the staff had been students of mine and were sympathetic with my situation. They believed in my innocence. Finally, someone other than my wife and lawyer believed in me. I hadn't recognized any of the guards when I first arrived because I stayed in my cell and refused to socialize.

It was suggested that I start studying anything and everything I could get my hands on. I agreed. I eventually became the research secretary to the N.A.A.C.P. I was learning how to do research in history and law. I joined the prison softball team and began to socialize like a normal human being. But I was still empty on the inside.

Without fail, Regina would visit me twice a month. Those few moments together charged my spirit which helped me deal with the loneliness I would have to endure once she left. The guards seemed to pick up on my depression and would go out of their way to help. They, on occasion, traveled to my house to pick up home-cooked meals for me. They even showed up with videos of my kids competing. I will always hold them in high regard for that. They definitely performed above and beyond the call of duty.

If you want to know what inadequacy feels like, try being in a cage watching your children grow up in front of your eyes. This was the hardest part for me.

Watching the tapes of my kids competing and going out for Chinese food afterwards gave me an idea. Since my dream was to teach, why couldn't I teach in here? The authorities, who were also my friends, agreed, so I started teaching classes to anyone wishing to attend. These training classes actually had a positive effect on the various gangs. I was teaching an unofficial class called "Kick Boxing Aerobics." Typically teaching a combative sport in a prison environment was looked down upon, but in a strange way, my classes were promoting peace. The various gangs were getting along with each other. Random violence was down. The Bloods, the Crips, the Detroit Boys, the Spanish mob, and all of the other gangs were sharing in a common interest: my classes. Everybody now had something in common, and I was the conduit who made the connection. It was pretty cool. Things were going well. I was serving what I would consider to be easy time.

During Regina's visits, she would update me on how the school was going. Apparently things were difficult. My being incarcerated more than doubled her workload. Once Regina gave birth to my fourth child, Antonio, she needed to slow down her daily obligations. She had to. Managing a school and four kids was enough to push anyone over the edge. I could sense the tension in my wife during our limited times together, but on the outside, she was strong and focused. I was torn up inside knowing what this prison thing was doing to my family. Eventually, she had to walk away from the school, which was a huge loss for Johnstown, my family, and my dream.

Seeing my kids getting bigger and growing without their father was the hardest thing I had to endure. The anger was trying to come back. That gnawing anger could either be used against me or for me. I decided to use it to my favor. I would be driven to succeed, and succeed I did. Among all the books I was reading, the Bible caught a certain interest in my inner core. I wasn't sure why I was being drawn to the Bible verses my Uncle Victor preached to me over and over again. Many nights I would fall asleep with an opened Bible upon my chest. Was I finding Jesus? Were Uncle Victor's words finally starting to sink in?

I began to study anything I could get my hands on, including books on business and theology. The business courses I read just confirmed what I already knew, but the religion stuff was amazing. Once again, I was a sponge absorbing the words, the meaning, and the spirit. I gained insights every time I picked up the Bible. I saw that there was no difference between a Christian and a true martial artist. It was all about discipline and faith. I started to see a clear picture of the spiritual battle being fought for my soul and other souls of the world. My upbringing and the hardships I had to endure now made perfect sense. My mother, my father, and yes, even my Uncles Victor and Nicky were understood like never before. Did I actually have to come to prison to have my heart softened by God? I think the answer was "yes." It was those lies that were told about me and my time in prison that would save my soul. I could see the irony. The Devil's blinders fell from my eyes, and I was left with a spiritual strength strong enough to cast him aside, and I did. The anger within me vanished, never to return again. I would fall asleep in prayer, repeating, "The Lord's my shepherd. I shall not want."

When I found out that I was eligible for early parole, I dropped to my knees and prayed thanks to God. Why didn't I listen to all those who tried to show me the way so many years earlier? When I entered the room to face the parole board, I saw myself looking eye-to-eye with the same judge who sentenced me five and a half years earlier. I took my seat and patiently waited for the proceedings to begin. I was self-confident, and I knew they could see it. God was shining through me, and that made me smile. Finally, the truth was told, heard, and believed. I was released within three days. As I walked out of there a free man, I contemplated, *If this is what walking with God was like, then I want in. I will kiss my kids as I tuck them in tonight. I will embrace Regina and love her as a man should love his wife. Praise God.*

A lot of people asked me if I was angry about what had happened to me. I smiled while I explained to them how the anger left me as soon as I allowed God to enter. When I added how I had the resolve to forgive my accusers, people thought I was exaggerating.

I contemplated a story I heard about an Amish family who had five of their children murdered by a crazed gunman. When the trial was over and the man was sent away to rot in a jail cell, the mother of the lost kids went to the convicted man's house and met his wife. They prayed together. Forgiveness was offered and accepted. I understood forgiveness and openly offered it. The fault wasn't with those parents who stole money from the fundraiser. There was no fault with the girls who lied about what I did or didn't do. The blame was totally on me for not listening to my Uncle Victor so many years ago. If only I had listened. I do think God wanted me to remain hard-hearted toward Him so he could teach me the lessons I needed to learn. I was ready now to be His warrior.

In retrospect, I was glad for the prison experience. I could now see that I needed that detour in my life so I could be humbled and brought before my Father, my savior, and my redeemer. It was now time to teach my family about my new dream—my spiritual journey. Tomorrow we would open our Bibles.

Matthew 6:14-15

Forgive people when they do wrong things to you. If you forgive them, your Father in heaven will also forgive you. But if you do not forgive them, your Father will not forgive you.

Chapter 17: Teach to Preach

I was over forty-five years old the day I finally tasted freedom. On the day of my release, Regina picked me up at the Newark Courthouse. There were no parades, no envelopes of cash for the wages I earned on the inside, nothing. At least in New York's prison system when you walked away from an institution, you received a few dollars for bus fare. In the land of the Klan, the only thing I walked away with was my appreciation for freedom, my desire to see my family, and my love for God. I guess you can say that the religious growth I experienced while on the inside was priceless. In that regard, I was now a wealthy man.

Once I was in the car with Regina, the nightmare was over. There was no reason to worry about yesterday. Yesterday was done. Tomorrow is tomorrow, and I can worry about it then. Today was a gift, so I wanted to bask in it. We stopped the car to smell, literally, the roses. It was good. As we made our way through Columbus, we passed through nice neighborhoods that slowly morphed into not-so-nice neighborhoods. I commented on how things have changed over the years. Everything was looking run-down and in need of maintenance. We continued driving and soon these below average hoods started changing into what looked like crack house neighborhoods. This was the neighborhood where our house sat patiently waiting. I was stunned and concerned, but I tried to smile on the outside for Regina and for the kids.

We entered the house. I could feel the tears fighting to be released when I first saw Crystal and Tiffany sitting on the couch in what looked like the smallest living room I had ever seen. My smile continued to camouflage my tears. They cried out loud and ran to me with open arms. We embraced for what seemed like an eternity. Antonio, seeing his big sisters balling, started to cry as well. Regina soon joined in. While basking in all of these tears, I wondered to myself, *Where's Louis Junior?* From behind I was engulfed in a bear hug death grip. My oldest son was now part of the circle of tears, and I was right in the middle of it. As soon as the group embrace subsided, I looked around one last time at the surroundings my family called home and said, "Go to your rooms and pack your bags. We're moving out of here as soon as possible."

Regina and I considered E.J. Swint, who had been with our school from the beginning, as a son, and our kids considered him a brother. Two days after my release, E.J. and I met downtown. He handed me $2500 cash and said, "This should help you get back on your feet."

He was right. The money really helped. It covered the cost of moving to the east side of Columbus to a place called Reynoldsburg, a much nicer neighborhood and, as you may remember, the neighborhood where I once thought I'd be managing a sandwich shop. The only problem with moving was the kids would have to leave their friends. Crystal took it harder than the others. I understood how she felt, remembering my childhood and the time when I had to move away from the Kingsborough Projects. Since God helped me get out of prison and helped me forgive those who did me wrong, I decided to pray about Crystal and the move and turn it completely over to Him. Crystal was still upset, but over the two weeks it took to get the move underway, she calmed down and eventually accepted the decision I made to relocate.

Prayer had done a lot for me since I found Christ, so I thought about what my needs were, made a list, sat down in a quiet place, and put it all to prayer. I asked for understanding from my family, continued forgiveness for all that was stained with blame, and for guidance on what I was going to do for a living.

When Regina gave birth to Antonio, she had to give up the school so she could focus on raising our four kids. Money was tight while I was locked up. I was so proud of how strong and determined my wife and kids were during these dark years. Tiffany stepped up to the plate by taking on babysitting jobs that would keep her out later than most 14 year olds. She would get home in time to clean up, get a little rest, and head off to school. She even took on a regular job at Kroger's market as a cashier, giving every penny she earned to her mom. What a saint. With all of this going on, she still found time to stay involved in various sports including martial arts. She occasionally taught at the Rick Moore Academy and eventually earned the title of a Martial Arts World Champion. To her siblings, she was the busy big sister and their second mom.

Louis Junior took the whole having-your-dad-in-prison thing really hard. He dove into a depression so deep that we all were concerned. He was not just on the edge, he was over it. For years, we were afraid he was lost in the vortex of his own demons. However, the day I was released, when he gave me that mighty bear hug, was the day his depression ended. My son was back from the dark side, praise God.

In contrast, Crystal and Antonio were too young to grasp the scope of my situation. All they knew was that they missed their

184 dad and were happy the day I came home. Praise God for the innocence of youth.

After Regina closed the school, she worked at a nearby day-care facility until the time I got out. She was able to keep the family together with her wages and the contributions from Tiffany. They had a roof over their heads, warm clothes on their backs, and food in their tummies. I thanked God those days were done. Now that I was a free man, it was time for me to take on the role of the breadwinner in the family. I wanted Regina to take a year off, a well-deserved break from her daily stresses of being the mom and dad. I wanted her to glow again as she did before I left (or should I say was taken away). I needed to find work immediately. However, who is going to hire an ex-con like me?

With my newfound spirituality, I had no choice: I had to turn it over to my faith in God. Up until then, I never really understood what the true meaning of faith was. This was going to be my crash course. I asked God to show me the path He wanted me on. I knew that whatever it was, it wasn't going to be easy. Nothing in my life was ever easy. This was the beginning of what would become my foundation of faith, a foundation I would learn to build my life upon.

We started by going to my Uncle Victor's Outreach for Youth program in Pataskala, Ohio. My immediate family attended church services there, so I was looking forward to seeing the expression on their faces once I showed up with my family in tow.

My cousin Steve lived on the church property and was being groomed to take over once Uncle Victor retired. Steve was so happy to see us. Apparently he and the rest of my clan had been praying for my salvation. It just goes to show what can be achieved with the power of prayer. John Kelly, a good friend and an elder at Outreach, told me about how Grandma Mymysayla used to pray for my soul. We were sitting in a park watching my son play ball as I was telling John about my plans to enter into a Bible school. Then he told me about how much faith my grandma had in me. He detailed how her knees developed calluses from her time with God.

"If only she could see you now," John praised. I smiled while nodding my head in agreement. For most of my life, my entire family was just waiting for that dreaded call—the one from a detective telling them that they needed to come down and identify my body. It was just a matter of time.

As we chatted, I pulled out a pack of smokes and started to light up. "Want one?" I offered. John declined. As the first exhale slowly drifted upwards, I watched as the cloud began to disperse in every direction. When I told John that I needed to quit, he agreed. Looking up at the rising smoke, he said, "When you speak the word of God, you speak with power, but if someone sees you smoking, the power of your words will disappear, just like that puff of smoke did."

John had a way of making me think. I started feeling like a hypocrite with each drag I took. This was God telling me to quit. That was my last cigarette, ever.

Cousin Steve ended up coming to my rescue. He offered me a car and a pocketful of cash to help me in my search for employment. I was grateful and humbled.

Armark, a local uniform service, was the first company to offer me employment. I accepted the job without hesitation. Cousin Steve became one of my advisors when I had matters of

186 a spiritual nature to deal with. Being a baby Christian, I had a fair share of questions to ask. Steve was always there for me, offering his advice. He was my teacher, and I was once again the student. Knowing Cousin Steve the way I did, including his past, I would often laugh thinking about how far this man had come, and here I was finally following him.

Steve was never a gangster, but his wild side was just that, wild. Previously, when Steve needed me, I was there. For example, when he told me about two thugs in his neighborhood who were trying to mess him up, I got pretty upset. Remember, in those days, I had some serious anger issues.

I went over to where these thugs were and before they could say or do anything, I whacked one of them on the side of the head with the butt of my handgun over and over again. After the fifth hit, this bully went down hard. His buddy didn't move for fear of what I would do to him. I thought this would be the last I would hear about these two dudes. Wrong! A few days later, Steve told me that they were now threatening him. They didn't care about who I was or what I could do to them. I rushed back to their house, kicked the front door open, and entered their living room. These guys weren't there. All I found was some of their family members sitting down for their evening meal. They froze as they watched me sit and wait.

I waited until one of my cousin's enemies finally came home. Once he arrived and not wanting to traumatize his family any more than I already had, I pulled him aside. With my gun firmly pressing against his ribs, I escorted him to my car. We were going for a ride, somewhere nice and quiet. We drove for a few miles until we were in a secluded part of town. There were no eyes or ears to interfere with the lesson I was about to teach him.

This guy was crying like a baby. He knew something bad was about to happen. For me, I had no idea of what was going to happen. I was going to leave his future and mine to the odds. It was time for a friendly game of Russian roulette. I removed all but one round from the cylinder and blindly gave it a good spin. His eyes widened. His brow was soaked with perspiration. I started by pushing the gun to my head, and without hesitation, I squeezed the trigger. *Click!* I lived. I smiled as I told him it was his turn. Spinning the barrel once more, I did the same to him. He cried while begging for his life. *Click!* He lived. It was my turn. *Click!* Then it was his turn again. *Click!* This was all it took. Class was dismissed. Steve never had trouble with these guys again.

Looking back now, I can see how little I cared for life—mine, his, and others. If you were a punk like me, you were expendable. Now that Steve had been saved by the Lord, I was happy to use him as my mentor. Who better to turn to than someone who understood me and knew about all of the skeletons in my closet.

When I got out of the Ohio state prison system, I was on fire for the Lord. It was a heat that I found bearable. I couldn't understand how I survived so many years without knowing Him. Questions were flooding my mind. *Why did I survive the assassination attempt? Why did those girls set me up for a nickel behind bars? Why did God take so long to show himself to me?* So many questions! I wanted to learn as much about theology as I could.

The one idea I had a hard time grasping was the concept that the closer you were to God, the more in your face the Devil was. Try to do anything good, and Satan will try to make you stumble, doubt yourself, bring up your past, find some way to tell you to stop, and remind you that you don't know what you are doing. I now recognize it was the Devil who sent me to prison, precisely when my school was doing so well. One day I had it all, and the next day I was reduced to a world within a five-by-ten cell. God watched the Devil at play with my soul and turned it to His favor. The Devil gambled with God—and lost!

My Uncle Victor's proudest moment was the day I called him and asked him to teach me about God. I didn't want the usual "study this or memorize that" kind of teaching. I was looking for the "stick-it-in-your-face" kind of spiritual truth that I knew only Victor could offer. I was ready for some serious growth. I needed growth. All I could think about was how my uncle never gave up on me. I wanted to look at life from a deeply spiritual perspective. I needed to be sure I would recognize the Devil if and when he returned for me. The first rule of a warrior was to know your enemy (and allies).

I started going to Uncle Victor's house on Monday evenings for Bible study classes. It was only the two of us and everything was going just great. I was closer to Victor than ever before. He felt pretty good about it as well. I knew he wanted to preach to me for years and now the day was his. All of the bad blood between us during my youthful years was long gone. When I looked at Victor, I didn't see that crazy man I once knew. Instead, I saw family, a man I loved and respected. It was a great time.

We would read a verse and then he would ask me what I thought it meant. I never did get it right. Once I answered with what I thought to be the inner meaning of the words, Victor would share his interpretation. I would try to see what he was trying to show me, but it never came in very clear. Then one day, I stopped thinking of myself as a human and instead started looking at myself as a child of God, a visitor on this earth. This was my magical moment. Everything changed for me as soon as my outlook changed. Reading scripture was now an entirely new experience, with a totally new meaning. I finally saw what Victor was trying to teach me. I wanted to read more, know more. I was hungry for it, and the hunger pangs would not go away. I was now at a level that my uncle could not satisfy. Uncle Victor had his outreach to run, so I sat down with Regina and told her of a new dream I had. She knew my dreams meant that there was no stopping me when I had my mind set on something, especially if it was important or life changing.

Regina and I both signed up for Bible college. It was an amazing time and sharing it together made it even more special. I learned how to apply discipline to my studies and to express myself more clearly. Regina learned how to understand me when I got deep into scripture. I was learning to preach, which made me nervous. Me, preach to the masses? I never saw that coming. God obviously had a plan.

I started attending different churches to expose myself to different styles of teaching. Some made sense to me, but others seemed to waste opportunity with their complexity and redundancy. Nevertheless, I loved their diversity. Then I started having dreams about what I was learning in Bible school. I told one of my professors about these dreams and he replied, "This is God speaking directly to your soul."

When I asked him why God preferred to speak with me at 3 a.m., my professor smiled at me, and with a deep understanding said, "You'll learn why soon enough."

It was eerie. Waking up at 3 a.m. with eureka moments was

190 driving Regina crazy. When I told her about my talk with the professor and what he said about God's speaking to me, I could see by the look in her eyes that she knew it was God all along. We were closer now than ever before. Regina finally glowed again.

The class was a small, intimate one. It worked well for what I needed in a classroom environment. The result of being shot in the head did prove to be challenging. I didn't process information the same way most normal people did. I needed concessions and they were offered without question. I was the only one in the class allowed to take open-book exams. Funny thing is that even with an open book, I would still pull in C's and D's, just enough to pass.

Victor once told me that when you speak God's word, scripture will come to you. He was right. Those who quote scripture with a smug demeanor, yet don't live a righteous life, don't impress me at all. They are phony, superficial. I'd rather talk with those who have experienced God's speaking directly through them and walk the walk.

With the grades I was pulling in, I was in need of God's intervention. My classmates were very supportive, giving me high praise for sticking with it and not giving up. Surrendering to God was now part of my DNA. God was my motivation; I was just going along for the ride. My dreams continued, and those 3 a.m. moments of realization became my favorite times of the night.

Jeremiah 1:5

Before I formed you in the womb I knew you, before you were born I set you apart; I appointed you as a prophet to the nations

Chapter 18: Dream Weaver

Here I was a reformed gangster with a colorful past, to say the least. I'd committed acts that I was ashamed of and tried to keep them buried deep inside where they couldn't surface and hurt anyone, especially those I love. And now here I was, a man of God, walking a spiritual path, one wrought with nightmares and dreams. I understood this to be the fight between good and evil, and my brain was the battleground. I had a front-row seat to something I preferred not to witness, but God wasn't going to let me off that easily.

At first, I couldn't believe that dreams could be God's way of speaking to me. I understood the nightmares were a tool to help me deal with pent-up guilt, but the dreams astonished me the most. Typically, when I would have a dream about my life before I was shot, I would stir in my sleep and wake up without any memory of my nighttime brain activity. But once my brain tissue was pierced, it was as if a portal was permanently opened. I was changed forever. Not only did I dream, but my dreams were also in brilliant Technicolor with every detail remembered the next day. They were like visions to me. I knew my professor was right when he told me that it was God speaking to me. Was I worthy? I didn't think so.

If the dream event was about some mundane activity, I simply filed it away in my memory bank for future reference, but when the dream involved Jesus, I was fully focused on each and every detail.

One of my first Jesus dreams occurred when Regina and I were attending Bible school. We were given an assignment to write a report about the synagogue leader Jairus and his dying daughter. Having two daughters of my own, I was able to feel Jairus' desperation when he asked Jesus to come and heal his child. Those feelings were the fuel for my dream. As my dream started playing out for me, I felt an overwhelming, desperate feeling. I found myself walking with Jesus. He was dressed in wrap-around fabric, and I was dressed more like Lawrence of Arabia than as a holy man.

While Jesus and I walked and talked, a crowd of people were following us from a distance. They were laughing and chatting and having a good time but still staying within ear shot and sight of the Messiah. The sun was burning hot, yet being near Jesus, we all felt comfortably cool. Suddenly out of nowhere, Jairus came running up to us, desperation in his face. His daughter was dying, so he knew Jesus was the only chance she had of recovery. I felt his anguish. Jesus immediately agreed to follow Jairus home. I stayed right beside Jesus as we made our way up the path towards the sick girl. The fear and desperation on the father's face ripped deeply into me. I cried for him and for all parents who have to watch their children suffer or die.

Abruptly, Jesus lost his step and almost fell to the ground. It was as if someone had pushed Him from behind. I reached out to catch him, and he quickly regained his balance. Jesus then turned around and said, "Hey, don't do that again. You almost made me fall!"

No one else heard Him. Then He turned to me as if I had been the one who tripped him and remarked, "Louie, what the heck?"

I immediately replied, "It wasn't me teacher."

I scanned the crowd behind us to see if I could find the one who was responsible. A young lady caught my attention. I knew she was the one. With a calming voice and outstretched hand, I approached her bleeding body, assuring her that she wasn't in trouble. I just wanted to know why she did it. She came forward and looked downcast as she said to Jesus, "I did it. I am truly sorry."

When she was asked why, she explained that she knew if she could only touch the hem on Jesus' clothing, she would be healed. Her faith was the driving force behind her actions. She talked about her illness, one that has inflicted her for over 12 years. Jesus placed his hands upon her head and whispered, "I know about your sickness and through your faith you have been healed. Go in peace, child."

We all watched as she went on her way with a youthful energy in her step. She was healed, and I got to see it personally. Jesus turned to me and asked, "Louie, what did you see?"

I replied, "I saw a young lady who desperately needed healing. She showed great courage to fight her way through a crowd while her body bled. Even though she was considered to be unclean, she was determined to touch you."

Jesus listened to my words. "Continue," he prompted.

"I explained to her how I understood her loneliness and embarrassment. I recognized her fatigue and exhaustion."

Jesus began to laugh loudly. Soon the entire crowd joined in, all laughing, and pointing their fingers at me as if I were some sort of joke. "You see, you don't understand," Jesus scolded.

I immediately stammered, "But she was so brave and desperate at the same time. Her faith is what healed her."

That comment just got Jesus and the crowd laughing louder and louder. The masses started chanting over and over, "He sees, but he doesn't understand! He sees, but he doesn't understand!"

I never felt so small and humble. Everyone turned and continued their way towards Jairus' house. The chanting continued. They left me sitting there on the sand, alone with tears gushing from my eyes. "He sees but he doesn't understand" could be heard as the crowd slowly disappeared over the hill without me.

I wiped my eyes as I woke up from my dream in a puddle of sweat. The clock read exactly 3 a.m., and the tears were still gushing. It was the sight of Regina sleeping beside me that snapped it all into perspective. This dream was heavy. It would take me a while to process it.

Unable to sleep, I decided to get up and go to my office for a little Bible study time. I had a collection of Bibles, each with a different way of saying the same thing. I loved the variety. When I had a dream involving Jesus, I knew that it was for a purpose: to teach me a lesson, to give me a message, or perhaps to plant the foundation for a sermon. I wanted to know why God planted that story in my head. What was the lesson? What was the message?

I began looking up any versus I could find that addressed bleeding women. Nothing was coming to me. I decided to give up on the verse search and focus on a word study. I started breaking down the content of my dream. What I found was astonishing. You see, when Jesus told the young lady to go in peace, what he actually said was, "Go in shalom."

Shalom takes the entire meaning to a whole new level. By her being healed by Jesus, she was now able to live a normal life. She could now be a contributing part of her community. No longer would she be shunned for being unclean. She could visit her friends, not having to be alone anymore. She and her surroundings were once again in harmony. This was the answer Jesus was looking for.

I now recognized the meaning of the dream. It had a multilayered meaning that started with me always being in the Word. I was not to become lazy; I must focus on the Word every waking moment of every single day. This was the only way I would beat the demons who kept trying to pull me back down. I also learned that I needed to have blind faith in Christ. I could't have a life of harmony without His standing beside me. Without Jesus, my life was nothing but a joke. This was what Uncle Victor meant when he said that without God and giving Him the glory, anything I did would have no meaning. And the last lesson I received from that strange and humbling dream was that I must always pray when study the Bible. If I asked my Father for guidance, I knew He would show me what it was He wanted me to see or learn.

After my graduation from Bible college, I continued my habit of visiting various churches. I wanted to expose myself to as many different styles of preaching as I could. Regina and I were trying to find a home church that shared my doctrine, but nothing was popping out at us. You would think that with all of the churches I'd een, at least one of them would be calling out my name. Nope. All f a sudden, the idea of letting God select my church came to me. I hould have turned it over to Him in the first place, but I was new o all of this and still had some growing to do. Thus, I lowered my ead and put our need for a home church to prayer. Less than three eeks later, I had a dream. It was one of those in-your-face dreams at left me exhausted and excited at the same time.

Jesus and I were walking through the desert talking about our journey together. Up ahead, I saw a man drowning people in a huge lake. I was overcome with despair as I turned to Jesus. He could see the sorrow on my face. I cried, "We need to go over there and stop that fool from killing all those people."

This guy was drowning boys, girls, seniors, adults, and yes, even babies. It was a horrific sight. I was becoming frantic with fear and empathy. I tried to run forward. I turned back urging Him, "Come on Jesus. We have to stop him!"

I was yelling my head off. Jesus, in his typical calming voice replied, "Don't worry about that man. He is doing a good job."

At that moment, I started thinking that Jesus was losing His mind. If those people were going to be saved, I would have to do it alone, without my Lord. As I tried to rush forward, my feet became extremely heavy. They wouldn't move. The harder I tried, the heavier they became. The more I struggled, the more I screamed and the more I screamed, the more Jesus smiled at me. This wasn' a dream; it was a dark and ugly nightmare. Then, while I continued my struggle for mobility, I saw my sister Madeline and her husband walking towards the lake with a picnic basket. They spread out the blanket, opened the basket, and removed all of the contents. They ignored the man in the water and all of the dead bodies floating face down. The murderer stayed there all night, killing. With the killing going on only five feet away from my sister, she invited Jesus and me to join them for lunch. I was convinced that everyone was out of their minds. Jesus smiled at me and suggested, "Let's go join Madeline and get something to eat."

Now this is where the nightmare gets weird. As soon a Jesu said, "Let's go," my feet were freed, and I was no longer on the lake's shore. I was now in the middle of the lake fighting to reach the surface and to reach air. I abruptly burst up from the depths of that lake, gasping heavily. I was alone in the water. When I looked towards the shoreline, I saw all of the people who had been "killed" standing there with Jesus, my sister, and her husband. Jesus had his arm around the man who did all of the killing. Jesus looked at me and said clearly, "This is your guy."

When I tried to focus in on that murder's face, I woke up. It was 3 a.m., and Regina was sleeping peacefully beside me. In the darkness of my bedroom, I pondered, *What does it all mean?*

The next morning was our day to try yet another new church. After our Sunday morning ritual of cooking, waking the kids, and doing everything else that needed to be done, we loaded up the car and headed out on our quest for the perfect church. Along the way, I detailed my dream to Regina. She knew it meant something special, but she had a hard time putting her finger on it. She was as baffled as I was. We agreed to leave it up to God to show us its meaning in His time, as He always did.

We parked the car and entered the new church. I nonchalantly looked around, as if I were giving them points for décor and ambience. Then I noticed the man up front standing behind the pulpit. Sweat started running down my face. I tugged at Regina's arm so hard I almost pulled her off of her feet. "That's him," I whispered loudly.

"That's who?" she cried while pulling free from my grip.

"The guy. You know, the man from my dream. The one who was drowning all those people."

My entire body broke out into a cold sweat. Regina was speechless. He was Pastor Dave DiYanni. I remembered visiting his church many months earlier when I was only interested in hearing different styles of sermons. However, at that time, Pastor DiYanni was on vacation, so why did his face come to me so clearly in my dream? I'd never seen this man before, not that I could remember. Why was Jesus endorsing him? Why did these dreams always happen at 3 a.m? I immediately prayed to God for wisdom. God gave me a simple answer: God knew this man and wanted me and my family to know him as well. I finished my prayer with thanks, and Romans 5:19 suddenly popped into my head:

For just as through the disobedience of the one man the many were made sinners, so also through the obedience of the one man the many will be made righteous.

From that moment forward, I surrendered myself to do whatever God wanted, even when it didn't make sense to me. The path He laid before me was the only path I wanted to be on. No exceptions.

The dreams continued. Sometimes their meaning was unclear and at other times they were clear as day. Eventually, Regina started having God dreams. She too was spiritually influenced by the Holy Spirit. I was glad to see her experiencing the same intense dreams as I was. If she ever had any doubts about my sanity, they were now put aside. She too was becoming a dream weaver like me.

Simply because I became a believer and had strange and beautiful Godly dreams didn't mean the Devil wasn't sitting on the sidelines waiting for his chance to pounce. When I look back at so many dreams I had regarding my spiritual healing, I never thought that through physical sickness I would find my greatest strength. It all began with a headache now and then. Then, I started feeling so lousy that I was in jeopardy of losing my uniform service job because of all of the sick days I would have to take. This was the first employer to offer me work after being released from prison, so I felt obligated to them. Taking sick days always made me feel awkward and guilty. Regina was telling me how poor my color was. She was concerned and for good reason. Initially, I thought the severe headaches were directly related to my old head injury.

Next, I experienced dizzy spells. I finally made an appointment with a doctor at the VA Hospital in Columbus. I described the chronic fatigue I was experiencing, no matter how much sleep I got. When they asked me if I had been thirsty, I described it as insatiable. It was at that moment I passed out. I went into diabetic shock and was becoming comatose. I was rushed to the VA facility in Chillicothe, a facility that was better prepared for the special type of care I would require. The doctors fought my coma for four days before getting it under control. When I woke up, I saw Regina and the kids in my room goofing around. It made me smile. Regina told me that she had been there for the past few days, but I was in no condition to remember anything after I passed out. The last thing I remember was speaking with the doctor back in Columbus.

I was diagnosed with Type 2 diabetes. The only means of control would be medications and a strict diet for the rest of my life. I was shocked and irritated. It was crazy.

After a few more days in the hospital, I was released with detailed instructions regarding what I and Regina would have to do to keep my diabetes under control. It was all about the blood sugar levels. I would have to check them regularly and self-inject insulin when they got out of whack.

I didn't do a very good job watching my blood sugar and had plenty of bad days, so eventually my employer had to let me go. I guess they just didn't want me going into a coma on their premises while I was on the clock. It's rather ironic that I nearly had to die before learning how much diabetes ran in my family. You would think that this would be something a mother would share with her son. As time passed, I did become better at managing my diabetes. However, from as far back as I could remember, I never liked needles.

I think my being unemployed is what prompted Regina to have one of her most meaningful spiritual dreams. This particular dream stirred within her mind for a long time before she actually mentioned any of the details to me. We were sitting in the kitchen enjoying an early morning cup of coffee when she looked deeply into my eyes and said, "Last week I had another one of those God dreams. He made a suggestion to me that I think might just work."

I leaned in towards her to absorb her every single word. She continued, "Why don't you create a magazine about the one thing you love?"

I immediately answered, "Karate?"

She nodded in agreement. This was the vision that God gave her. After thinking about it for seven days and reflecting upon the commercial art classes I had taken in prison, it all seemed so natural, as if it was meant to be. I was excited about the idea; nevertheless, I decided I would pray about it. I didn't merely pray, but instead I went into what I called "super-prayer" mode where my every waking moment was spent in conversation with God.

Why wasn't God presenting himself to me as he usually did? The idea of being in super-prayer mode but not getting an answer was foreign and unnerving. The only thought that kept coming to me during my intense prayers was the memory of a great man, the late Master Roy Taylor from Sentry Martial Arts. He was truly one of those special people you may run into only once or twice in a lifetime. When Regina and I were starting out with our own school, Master Roy gave us $3500 worth of products to use for our grand opening. Once the Johnstown school was up and running, repaying Master Roy was our top priority. We never got our supplies from anyone else from that moment on. When he died, he left a lot of people behind who were touched by his kind spirit. He was a loving and compassionate martial artist. Then it dawned on me. Master Roy used to have a magazine named Ohio Martial Arts. Why didn't I see the connection earlier? Was this God speaking to me?

When I checked the registry on use of *Ohio Martial Arts Magazine, Incorporated*, I found that the name was available. Regina's dream and vision were coming true. I filed all of the legal papers and registered the name Ohio Martial Arts Magazine, Inc. in honor of Master Roy, my friend and mentor. The foundation of the magazine is based upon Matthew 22:3:

Thou shall love thy neighbor as thyself.

To us, it meant to serve those less fortunate. We lived by those words. We spent our days visiting the elderly and helping them with their shopping and other chores. We also spent a lot of time organizing food and clothing drives. For kids who couldn't afford to go to tournaments, the magazine offered them scholarships. However, finding the money for these projects was challenging. Even though we had a 501(c)(3) non-profit status, not enough corporations were willing to invest or donate to our cause. If God planted this magazine into Regina's mind, then He had a long-term goal for it; He just hadn't let us in on His plans yet. That was okay. We could wait. Until that day, we would continue with our

202   magazine and the classes we taught at our church. Some students would train at the regular rate and others could train for free. I was positive Regina or I would soon have a dream showing us the answer. I was eager.

Daniel 8:15

When I, Daniel, had seen the vision, I sought to understand it. And behold, there stood before me one having the appearance of a man.

Chapter 19: The Crazy Reverend

Starting a magazine not only consumes an enormous amount of time but also devours financial resources with an insatiable appetite. The *Ohio Martial Arts Magazine* was blessed the day I met with Keith Ciotti and Annette Gall. It was when we first started the publication back in 2009 when Keith offered to assist us financially. Being the general manager of Fort Rapids, an indoor water park in Columbus, Ohio, Keith was keen on investing in our future and the future of our community. If we ever needed a place to hold a tournament or if we encountered unexpected expenses (and there were plenty), Keith and Annette were always there. They were two angels sent to me from heaven. At 50 years old and taking on this new venture, I needed all the help I could get. I prayed thanks for them many times.

One day while I was doing some shopping at the Whitehall Walmart, another angel came into my life. I was helping one of the elderly ladies who came to depend on me and my students to help them with their simple errands. I was having such a great time watching the expression of joy wash across her face. Not only did she have some shopping needs, but she was also lonely. I was helping her on many levels, and I was being blessed for it. As we walked up and down the aisles, she openly told me about her family. She was the primary caregiver for her granddaughter. This child had to move in with her the day her mom and dad decided to make heroin their highest priority. As we were chatting, Leonard Kinzel, the store manager, approached us and asked us if we were finding everything we needed. I really appreciated his hands-on customer service approach, and next thing I knew, the three of us were deep in conversation. When Leonard asked me about my profession, I eagerly bragged about my *Ohio Martial Arts Magazine* and how we were working to help our local community. He hung onto every word. Leonard offered to see what his Walmart could do and said he would be in touch. I gave him my card and we started towards the checkout counter. My elderly friend looked at me and said, "He's such a nice boy." I agreed,

To be perfectly honest with you, I didn't expect to hear from Walmart. I did toy with the fantasy of how cool it would be to have a giant store chain like the Walmart Corporation as a financial contributor, but being a realistic kind of guy, I realized it was only a dream, and not one of those "God dreams." After a month passed, I got a call from my new Walmart friend. Leonard wanted to know how his employer could help. I immediately went into my promotional mode detailing out how their sponsoring our tournaments would help out in a big way. His voice started getting nervous as he expected me to say that we attend five, six, or even more tournaments a year. Leonard asked how many and I told him two. I also added that we work with local veterans in raising funds to help families who have a hard time paying their bills. Walmart agreed to partner with us and for the next year, *Ohio Martial Arts Magazine* and Walmart walked together, hand in hand.

It was a sad day when my Walmart friend Leonard Kinzel decided to relocate to Florida. This ended our Whitehall store sponsorship. His replacement wasn't very community minded. I started asking myself why God would take away this windfall. What was the purpose? It was time to return to the super-prayer

mode. I loved it when God had a plan, even though I was not
always in the loop as far as the details go.

Looking at the possibility of having other Walmarts sponsor
us, especially now that the Whitehall store had set a precedent, I
made an agreement with the Reynoldsburg store. Tony Crosby, a
former Whitehall Walmart shift manager, was recently promoted
to co-manager at the Reynoldsburg store. He knew all about the
Ohio Martial Arts Magazine from his days working with Leonard
Kinzel. Tony believed in our cause and did all he could to help us
out.

Tony's contribution was helpful, but we still needed more. At
least it showed us that we were heading in the right direction. God
was once again showing me the path, and all I had to do was follow.
God gave us the Reynoldsburg store as a teaser. He wanted us to
hit the pavement and to have face-to-face conversations with as
many Walmart stores as we could. Regina and I did just that. As we
worked the regional stores, I had a prayer team doing what they did
best: pray. We searched for over 18 months before finding that one
door that would swing open for us. Funny as it seems, we thought
God was pointing us towards Walmart retail stores. Who knew that
He was actually sending us in a different direction altogether? A
meeting was set up with Mike Wieburg, the vice president and
general manager at the Walmart Distribution Center in Grove
City, Ohio. After listening to my pitch, he sat back, intertwined his
fingers, and remarked, "How can we help you with your needs?"

As I threw out some numbers at him, he smiled and replied,
"We're in."

With that said, Walmart, through its distribution center, became
a major sponsor for the community.

I always refer to the Walmart Corporation as the store with a heart. Most large corporations would help out those large charity organizations who offer publicity in return. Here was Walmart, willing to take a chance on a small venture like *Ohio Martial Arts Magazine* with interest in only one thing: helping out the community. Now, I will always do my shopping at Walmart. Whenever I am invited to speak at a church or other gathering, I make sure to include talking about the relationship between Walmart and the *Ohio Martial Arts Magazine*'s program. I begin with a summary of our mission statement followed by the line, "Thank God for Walmart, the company with a heart!" I'm telling you, that is a real attention grabber.

I was blessed to have two other companies jump onto our sponsor bandwagon. Columbus Office Solutions and Columbus Executive Solutions became part of the *Ohio Martial Arts Magazine* (OMAM) family. It all started the day Bill Sopher, the owner of Columbus Office Solutions, approached me and asked many questions about what we were doing. The minute he brought up God, that was it. He and I created a powerful bond. We talked for hours. He was able to recognize what God was doing in my life, and I saw what the Lord was doing in his. We both wanted to work towards bettering our community, so my magazine was going to be the way we would both achieve our goals.

Bill made a call to arrange a meeting with Chris Gordon, another Godly man who happened to own Columbus Executive Solutions. I know many men who call themselves "Christians" and can talk the talk, but Chris also walks the walk. I was impressed. We all became great friends. We were now receiving more financial assistance and our printing needs were being met as well. It was all coming together. God continued to amaze me.

Knowing how my wife, my daughter Tiffany, and I had to

struggle to pay our magazine bills, we needed to find a grant writer who could do his or her magic and yet be willing to work for little or no income. We needed someone who would be able to act like Biblical Rahab who thought only of her goal, not the journey to get there. Rahab was saved because she acted on what she believed. When Joshua sent his two spies into Jericho, it was Rahab who opened up her house offering the spies protection. God chose Rahab and because of her willingness to help, her house and all in it were saved. We needed a Rahab to join our team.

We looked at some people who said they would write grants for us, but sadly, they did not follow through. The need would continue, so if it weren't for the generosity of our corporate sponsors, we would have been in trouble long ago. A steady source of the magazine's income was from the martial arts' classes we held at our church. Those who could pay paid, but those who were poor didn't have to pay. This was our way of conducting business, and God saw to it that our financial needs were met. We felt blessed to be able to pass onto others what God had graced us with.

With my connections with gangsters and other undesirables, you can imagine the reputation I made for myself in Columbus with moms and dads. I was being hailed as the "Crazy Reverend," and I wore that title with pride. It all started when I went to the darkest parts of town where the drug addicts and prostitutes hung out. Wherever you find addicts and hookers, you are sure to find pushers and pimps. They all knew me, and I knew them. With my background, there wasn't one of them who intimidated me. God wanted me to minister to these broken kids as Uncle Victor ministered to me. If they wouldn't come to the House of God, I was going to bring the House of God to them.

When I told Regina I was going to "church" on the north side of town, she would become nervous. One day I made the mistake of taking her with me; she actually thought I was going to a real brick and mortar church. You can imagine the surprised look on her face when I pulled up into the heart of the Columbus ghetto and approached a group of tough-looking characters sitting on a stoop looking for trouble. While I preached, Regina couldn't keep her eyes off the booze, drugs, and guns that surrounded us. I never gave it a second thought.

Now when I left the house to go to church on the north side of town, Regina was concerned about my safety. I guess I could see her point. After all, she was the one who sat in the hospital day after day watching her husband and the father of her children clinging on to life. The five bullet holes that long ago morphed into ugly scars reminded her that she should be afraid. But should I have been afraid? I didn't think so. I walked with Jesus—remember my dreams?

To this day, Regina cooks food for me to take to these north side church services where everyone devours every last bite. This is her gift to our ministry. The kids I ministered to, while licking their fingers clean, would threaten to take Regina away from me so she could cook for them full time. Joking and laughing hysterically they remarked, "Don't worry preacher, God will get you another woman."

While In some ways I found them funny, in other ways, well let's just say that without Regina, I would be but a shadow of who I am.

Evangelizing to the gang members in our community and showing them that some of us didn't automatically cast them off as lost causes had a profound effect for good. No matter how hard the Devil tried to sway public opinions against our mission, we were blessed in doing God's work. After all, who did Jesus minister to? *209* He ministered to the unclean and social outcasts, to those who had the greatest need.

I continued with my magazine and my street ministry; the Devil continued to throw obstacles onto my path, so I had to watch myself every step of the way. His latest attempt to thwart my journey with God was more irritating than incapacitating. My irritant was a guy in town who I liked to refer to as the "ham-burglar" ("ham" for the pig he is and "burglar" for his attempt to steal our gift to our community). He called Pastor DiYanni and told him that he had some insider information about me that he needed to bring to light. He referred to it as "FYI stuff." Because Pastor DiYanni was intrigued, he agreed to set up a meeting. When Pastor DiYanni asked me if I wanted to sit in on the meeting, I replied, "Of course."

If I was doing something wrong, I wanted to know about it so I could take corrective action. Although no matter how hard I looked at what I was doing, I could see no wrong, only blessings.

I arrived at the church a few minutes ahead of schedule, but I decided to give the ham-burglar enough time to tell his story to the pastor before I entered. I stayed out of sight until the time was right. Fifteen or twenty minutes after the meeting started, I gently knocked on pastor's door and entered. Once he saw me, my accuser's face went pale. Then Pastor DiYanni asked him to repeat his allegations. He started spewing his lies once again, but this time his face changed from ashen to blood red. I listened to each lie, allowing him to finish before saying anything. He brought up my prison record, my gangster beginnings and affiliations, and how I was almost killed in a blazing gun battle. He also accused me of currently being in parole violation. Most of what he said

210   was true, except for the part about my being in violation of parole. I allowed him to finish. When he was done, I asked Pastor DiYanni if I could offer my rebuttal, and he said, "Of course."

First, I said, "Brother, allow me to tell you why they call me the 'Crazy Reverend.' Everything you said is true, except for the parole thing. I am not on parole. I do not have any parole restrictions, so I can come and go as I please. As for the other stuff, yup, been there, done that!"

His jaw dropped as I continued with my lecture. Pastor DiYanni looked on with a smile on his face. The next words that came out of my mouth were God's words, not mine. The words flowed like a torrent river, "I'd like you to know that Luke 6:41 clearly says,

'How can you say to your brother, Brother let me take the speck out of your eye, when you yourself fail to see the plank in your own eye? You hypocrite, first take the plank out of your eye and then you will see clearly to remove the speck from your brothers eye.'"

I was now in full preaching mode, and there was no holding me back. As the ham-burglar tried to insert an opinion here or there, I continued without interruption until I was done saying all I had to say. I couldn't believe that this guy was proclaiming to be a Christian and was at one time a Godly member of this very church. I asked him, "Do you know what it is that I do for a living or what kind of man I've evolved into?" Before he could utter a reply, I firmly added, "Of course not." I asked, "Then tell me now why you would speak such lies about me and try to destroy God's work?"

With his head hung low, he searched for the words that would justify his actions. None were found. All he heard was the truth open and on the table, for all to see. The truth is that I was once a bad man, and now I am not. It was as simple as that.

There was something about my being the Crazy Reverend that Pastor DiYanni loved. He saw me as being unique in more ways than one. When I looked at myself, I saw a man with flaws. But then again, there is documented evidence about men with flaws being used for God's glory: Paul persecuted Christians, King David was a womanizer, and Noah, well this guy could even drink me under the table! When Jesus came into my dream and told me that DiYanni was my man, I knew there was something special going on. Pastor DiYanni forgave me for my sins just as my Father did.

Being who I was and doing what I did, I realized that I would always be an easy target for Satan's wrath. All I could do was to forgive as others had forgiven me. The ham-burglar was easy to forgive. His actions weren't his fault. The Devil used him as a puppet, pulling his strings. I feel sorry for those who think they are doing the right thing when in reality they are doing the Devil's work. A pastor once told me that just because one has the "right" to do something doesn't mean that it is the "right" thing to do. He was describing the ham-burglar and his actions to a tee. The mission that God had given me would not slow me down, no matter how hard the Devil tried to interfere. With God on my side, who could be against me?

Job 4:12

A word was secretly brought to me;
my ears caught a whisper of it.

Chapter 20: Reflections

The day I faced my accuser (ham-burglar) was one that I cherished for all the right reasons. It wasn't a matter of facing my enemy and winning the confrontation. Although I did win and Pastor DiYanni praised me for how I handled the situation, I wasn't looking for glory and notoriety. It wasn't about anything other than giving the glory to God and leaving it up to Him to guide me and my words and to overflow my veins with the blood of forgiveness and understanding. Ham-burglar faded into the sunset, not as a hero, but instead as a defeated man. I felt his pain. A younger me would have basked in his misery.

Events happen in life for a reason. I am convinced of that. If one blesses others, then he or she will also be blessed. The Bible is very clear about how one must give in order to receive. I liked to give without expectation of receiving. After all, it wasn't about me. If I needed an answer, I knew exactly where to search. Super-prayer mode was my secret weapon. When I was in super-prayer mode, people who didn't know me would think of me as being strange and unsettling. After spending fifty-three years on this earth, I was beyond the point where I really cared about what others thought about me and my ways.

When I look back over the years, it amazes me that I am still here to do His work. Why wasn't I dead? There was only one reason my life was spared: I still had work to do on this earth. It seems

214   that when God wants you, he wants you. Not only did God give me insight, but he also used my hardcore upbringing as a means for giving me the inner strength I needed in order to do His work. Without it, I would be surrendering under the insurmountable pressures of street gang ministry. My Uncle Victor's beatings gave me a resolve and determination to face my enemies, no matter how mighty they might seem. For example, look at David. Do you think Goliath intimidated him? I am sure he did, but that didn't stop little David from picking up that rock and flinging it at his foe with his sling. God took care of his aim.

How could someone like me survive the Brooklyn Projects or the state prison system without the grace of God? It couldn't happen. No one is that "lucky." Because God's grace was so overflowing, I was carried through my entire youth without ever knowing it. How else could you explain my mother's walking right into the middle of a rumble, finding me, and dragging me off by the ear? It was God. When my anger and revenge led me right into the hands of the entire rival gang whose intent was to kill me, I do know that if I had been any other kid, I would have been destined to a plot six feet under. At that time, I was too stupid and hard hearted to see it for what it really was. Even the dog-sized rats that tried to eat my flesh weren't enough to keep me down. Although God was holding my hand every step of the way, I was ignorant of His presence. I was hard hearted.

I am now a full grown fifty-three-year-old man who sees God clearly and who has a personal relationship with Him. Only now when I look back do I recognize the angels who were with me at those years. As a young rebel I continued to resist, but these angels blessed me anyway. At twenty-three, they allowed my path to cross with Regina's, so my life's journey would never be a lonely one again. I found my true soul mate who loved me when most women would have run away. For the next ten years, I was blessed with amazing children, all of whom I raised differently from the way I was raised. I had plenty of love to give, so with each child born my love bank increased tenfold. I was twenty-five when Louis Junior was born, twenty-nine when Tiffany burst into this world, and thirty-three when I watched Crystal's head pop into view. Then at 40, Antonio, my youngest son, graced our family. Sadly, I would miss his birth while serving time for something I didn't do. That was the second time I had gone behind bars for someone else's crime. That was the time in my life when God made Himself known to me. It wasn't until I was in my 40s that I finally began to see after being blind for so many years. I was forty-five when I was finally offered an early release from prison. The truth about my innocence was finally known. Yes, God does work in mysterious ways and in His own time.

Another miracle happened when I was back on the streets, and every tangible thing I had created was gone. Regina and I had to start from scratch, but that was okay with me. I would rebuild my life, one brick at a time, but this time it would be bigger, stronger, and better. My ministry would focus on the street or wherever I was needed. Sometimes I would be delivering a sermon in a slum to thugs and, at other times, I would be standing in front of the masses, amazed that they would be interested in listening to what a thug like me would have to say.

My sermons carried the same message: believe in the miracles that you cannot see. Also, tithe in abundance. Give until it *hurts*. There are people I would refer to as "cowards." They have no faith as far as tithing goes. They, with a guilty smile, pass the collection tray without contributing. They are money hoarders who think only of themselves and not the needy who would benefit from their gift. Even though the Bible is clear about giving the top ten percent back to God, I feel strongly that the ten percent mentioned is not a carved-in-stone amount. Instead, it is only a guideline which means if you can afford 20 percent, give it. God will provide for your needs. Remember the Bible verse that talks about how if God provides all that the birds need to survive, surely he would do the same for you. Are you not more important to God than birds? It is because of the faithful Christians who regularly tithe that churches are built, Bibles are published, and missionaries are able to travel around the globe doing God's work. It is my experience that when you give in abundance, He blesses you in abundance. Isn't that what it is all about? Although my spiritual growth came with a very high price tag, Jesus paid for my salvation, in full, the day he was hung upon the cross.

Now that the magazine was growing and the memory of Master Roy was preserved in the magazine's name, Regina and I were able to catch our breath. Our community programs were popular because they reached people who needed financial, emotional, and spiritual help. We were right where we wanted to be. We were on the battlefield, in the trenches, facing the Devil head on. Our weapon was His word, so we were fighting like mighty warriors being lead by Gabriel himself. Regina, my kids, and I all believed the same truth—OMAM was God's conduit into the hearts and minds of those who were searching. If one were lost, all he or she had to do was reach for our outstretched hands. We were there for anyone who needed us. OMAM became my church and the community my congregation.

As each day continued to pass and routine settled in, I took joy in reflecting upon those who had a significant impact on my life. I would find myself reflecting on the precious gift of knowing them. My cousin Aaron Torres used to call me "Pito" (the Spanish word for whistle). Apparently he thought I looked like a whistle when I was born. When I became older and streetwise, Cousin Aaron loved walking with me around the streets of Brooklyn. He was in awe knowing that I was a tough-as-nails gangster, feared by all. He would always feel safe walking with me. I was so pleased to see him grow into a Godly man. He is now one of the many that I seek out when I find myself in need of spiritual guidance. He is one of my many rocks.

Uncle Nicky was the one I saw as a hero from as far back as I could remember. He always stood tall and strong and those near him feared him, as they should. I never feared him because I never really recognized his ugly side. All I ever saw was his kindness and love. Others experienced his anger and intimidation. It is ironic that today the only one who sees his anger and intimidation is Satan. Others who really know him can only see the spark I saw as a child: his love for his fellow man and his admiration for God. Uncle Nicky is a walking miracle.

Uncle Victor is one for the books. Here is the guy who probably had the most profound impact on the man I am today. I can remember being held up by my neck, my feet dangling below me, and knowing that a beating was coming my way. Those were dark days for me, dark days indeed. As with Uncle Nicky, Victor had an angry beast deep within him. The main difference between my two uncles was that Nicky knew how to control that

218 beast while Uncle Victor's beast controlled him. Sadly, on many occasions I found myself in the middle of his inner conflicts. Eventually, he conquered the beast, and Uncle Victor was reborn. He became a spiritual influence on others like me. Even though I never recognized it at the time, most of what he said sank in. I like to believe that his constant preaching slowly softened my heart and finally allowed the Holy Spirit to enter me. Everything Uncle Victor flung at me was true, but I was too stubborn to know it, see it, and feel it.

My mother, well, I guess one can say she had an impact on me as well. Like my father, my mother taught me some valuable lessons I carry with me throughout my life. When I look back at my upbringing, I can truly say that today I am a better husband and father because of my parents. My father has long been out of the picture, but the memory I have of him is as fresh as can be. My mother, on the other hand, is still a part of my life and is an amazing grandmother to my kids. Regina has taken motherhood to an entirely different level compared to my mother. I guess I lived my childhood days during a different era. We were all different people, but some of us just never changed.

Besides family, there were so many others who helped mold me into the man I am today. They were the potters, so I was nothing more than a clump of wet, soft clay. One of the potters who stands out is Pastor Mark Poland. This man advised me on every aspect of my life, and I mean everything. When I felt unworthy, Pastor Mark would reassure me that my purpose was clear and I should not worry about anything other than allowing God to use me in any way He saw fit. If I felt nervous about a speaking engagement, Pastor Mark would talk to me about the gift I have, the gift of communication. If I thought my preaching style didn't feel right, he would remind me that my rough edges reflect the strength of God's warriors, and my tough demeanor was simply passion. Whenever I needed someone to pray for me or my cause, Pastor Mark Poland was always the first one in line. This man is obviously one of God's angels sent down to watch over me.

Proverbs 3:9

Honor the Lord with your wealth,
with the first fruits of all your crops.

Chapter 21: That Little Chair Behind the Pulpit

I had so many people praying for me and with me. I kept asking myself, "Am I worthy?" The answer was always the same, "No," but for whatever reason, God felt differently. He had a plan for me, and I was willing to blindly follow. I evolved into the spiritual man I am today for a reason. So much good has happened to me over the years. There are too many blessings to count. Why does my Father give me so much?

My life has now come full circle, yet I am still lost within the memories that haunt me. Only now can I begin to use the ugliness of my past to solidify the beauty of the here and now. I feel empowered. Like the caterpillar changing into a brilliantly beautiful butterfly, I stand tall and reach up towards the heavens as if trying to stretch out my wings. I find myself reflecting upon each blessing and miracle as I lift my head and with all I have I shout with an overpowering joy, "Hallelujah!"

My voice echoes throughout the immediate area. The loudness of the Holy Spirit flowing from my cry startles me. I opened my eyes and looked quickly to the left and to the right. God was no longer showing me my life's journey. I was stunned as my work suddenly came into focus. Here I was standing up next to that lone chair, off stage behind the pulpit. God had let go of my hand, but I knew he was still there with me. As the organist played the last hymn for the morning, she looked over her music sheet towards me to catch a glimpse of the outspoken man who was overcome with the Holy Spirit. I quickly sat down, embarrassed. My mind was now filled with images of Reverend Nathaniel Johnson speaking recently at the Baptist revival, overflowing my heart with the Holy Spirit, and baptizing my soul with His word.

God had taken me so far back into my life that I lost all recollection of where I was and why I was there. I suddenly remembered where I was when Preston Moore popped his head through the curtain saying, "Get ready. You're up next."

I was at the Perry Chapel Baptist Church sitting on that single chair behind the pulpit. It was all coming back to me now. I remembered how God answered my question regarding why I was there with a firm, "You don't know them like I do."

This was the moment that I heard my name being announced. People were applauding loudly; it was thunderous. My knees were shaking, and there was a loud nervous thumping within my heart. I made my way up to the pulpit. As I looked around at all the expectant faces, I pondered that I didn't feel comfortable doing this. I still wanted to run away and hide. I inhaled one last time, said a quick, "Hallelujah," and with that, the room went wild. God took over from that very moment. My sermon began.

When I spoke, they hung onto every one of God's words, offering "amens" and "praise God" throughout the entire sermon. I was having an out-of-body experience. It was as if I were standing in the wings watching myself from a distance. As I watched myself deliver the sermon, I became overjoyed, thinking, *Praise God for this day.* This sermon was yet another crossroads for me. I concluded and slowly stepped to the side of the pulpit. A tear formed, then two, and then the floodgates opened. The thunderous

applause and standing ovation told me that they understood. I *223*
believe that this was God's way of saying to me, "Good work my
son. I am pleased!"

I thanked Him for holding my hand and reminding me of
where I came from, for showing me my life, my legacy, and my
crossroads.

Romans 5:19

*For just as through the disobedience of the one man the many
were made sinners, so also through the obedience of the one man
the many will be made righteous.*

Epilogue

Some would think this to be the end of my story, but I would argue that it has only just begun. When I look back at the journey of creating this book, I praise God for giving me the strength to deal with each and every obstacle I found on my path, and there were many.

For years, Christians and non-Christians have encouraged me to put my story to pen. I would smile and agree, but the spark needed to start the process was never there. I put the notion that anyone would be interested in reading my story on the back burner, to be forgotten, ignored, and avoided. Still they argued that my biography would help those who were in need of spiritual guidance and help them find the answers they were searching for.

I still relied on that back burner as a storage place for things I didn't want to deal with. This avoidance was just another one of the Devil's stumbling blocks he placed before me. He was betting on my tripping. For years he would win his wager at my expense.

Then one day someone who brought up the "write a book" idea said to me, "Since you were forgiven for your sins, don't you think that others deserve the same forgiveness?"

I quickly answered with reverence, "Yes, of course."

This was the moment I realized why my story needed to be told. I had to show that it really didn't matter what I may have done, God forgave me, unconditionally, and I was a shining example of

226 His mercy.

Now that the book idea was finally off the back burner, I was still faced with the fact that I knew nothing about writing a book. I knew that my Uncle Nicky once wrote a best seller about the darkness of gang life on New York's streets and how he was saved. David Wilkerson—that strange white preacher from Pennsylvania—came to my neighborhood and brought the Holy Spirit to my uncles. He wrote a well-known book entitled *The Cross and the Switchblade*. Certainly writing a book about my journey was a possibility. But where do I start? I didn't know the answer.

God, as usual, placed the answer right in front of me. Through my involvement with the *Ohio Martial Arts Magazine*, I met a lady named Lin. We started talking one day, and when she told me that she worked for a publisher, I immediately told her the one line that she had probably heard a thousand times before, "I've got an idea for a book."

I really thought that this would lead to nothing more than a conversation. She asked me for a short synopsis, and as I started explaining the details of my past, her interest was obviously sparked. Before I could finish my story she interrupted, "I know the perfect person to write your story, and he is a Godly man just like you. Let me give him your contact information, and we'll see where it goes from there."

I didn't expect to hear anything. I was never so wrong. God was reminding me how to have faith.

As time passed, I actually forgot about the book project. I was busy dealing with the day-to-day responsibilities of the magazine. Then one day, out of the blue, I got a call from some guy who introduced himself as Richard Hunter. At first, I was trying to

figure out what he was selling, but I soon realized he was the
biographer Lin told me about. I became excited, feeling like a
child on Christmas Day. Richard was interested in my story and
was willing to listen to what I had to say. We talked for almost
two hours before he started explaining the process and timeframe
for this sort of undertaking. I heard everything he said, but not too
much of it was sinking in. I was just too excited about this book
actually becoming a reality. Richard wanted to make sure I was
comfortable with his type of writing style before we entered into
an agreement. He mailed me two of his already published books
and suggested that I call him after I read them. I already knew he
was the right man for the job, but I was happy to receive his books
and eagerly waited for their arrival.

When I started reading Richard's book *Will Work 4 Food*, I had
a hard time handling the theme of the book. This book deals with
homelessness in Tucson, Arizona. It is a series of mini-biographies
all told by homeless people. It was a little too close to home for me.
I saw myself in every story I read in that book, so I was intimidated.
But I did like Richard's writing style and eagerly started moving
forward with the project.

As the interviewing started, I was amazed at how much my life
was like an onion, each layer being peeled back one at a time. Each
time a new layer was exposed, I would have to face the ugliness of
my earlier years. I began having nightmares. God was showing me
exactly who I was. Even my kids, after hearing the first couple of
chapters, begged me not to make them read any more. They didn't
want those old wounds reopened. At one point, I got so depressed
that I decided to put the book on that back burner. I was done with
it. I was beginning to doubt my own salvation.

The day I called Richard to tell him I wanted to go no further with the project was the day God brought me back into the light. Richard was not at home, so I started talking with his father-in-law, John"Acy"Campbell III ("Red"). When I told him why I called, he shared his experience in telling the story of his life in *Where Eagles Fly, Remember Me...* This was one of the books Richard had sent me.

As an American, Red was an R.A.F. fighter pilot who flew Hurricanes during WWII with various Eagle Squadrons. After being shot down in the South Pacific, Red spent the remaining three-and-half years of the war as a Japanese POW on Java. When Richard was doing the interviews for the book, Red experienced similar nightmares to those I had experienced. Red and I had a very interesting bond; he knew my pain and fear. Thus, after speaking with Red, I found the strength to continue on with my book. Red was not only a hero during the war, but he is also now my hero for helping me deal with my own monsters.

Regina, even though she too hated the memories of those ugly days, insisted that I continue working on the book. She would review the chapters and add her commentary, share in a laugh, and yes, share in a tear as well. She would tell me this book wasn't about me or us; it was far bigger than we were. It was all about God and His will for His children. Regina sacrificed so much over the years and continues to do so.

John 3:30 says clearly, "He must increase, but I must decrease." This verse puts my entire journey into perspective, and for that I am grateful. Far too many people go through life without seeing the clarity of God's will. My heart aches for them. My path is right there for all to see; everyone is welcome to join me along my path.

As I hold out my hand, it is up those who need guidance to reach 229 out and take hold. I will guide them as my Father has guided me. Therefore, when I am asked if this book's last chapter is the end, I reply, "How could it end now? There is so much more for me to do."

Please stop by my website at http://ohiomartialartsmagazine. com to learn what my ministry is all about. We are dedicated to the advancement of martial arts everywhere, and unlike most martial arts publications, ours is first and foremost a God-focused, non-profit publication. My entire family is devoted to the *Ohio Martial Arts Magazine*. Any contribution you can spare would make a huge difference. With the ongoing needs of our center, every penny you can donate would help.

Proverbs 11:25

Whoever brings blessing will be enriched, and one who waters will himself be watered.

Ohio Martial Arts Magazine Inc.
P.O. Box 712
Reynoldsburg, Ohio 43068
(740) 919-0700

About the Author

Born and raised in Montreal, Quebec, Canada, R.S. Hunter always longed for a life somewhere warm and inviting. After serving with the Royal Canadian Air Force, he ventured west to Victoria, British Columbia, seeking his dream. The weather was much better, but not enough palm trees for his liking. He now lives in Tucson, Arizona, where there are over 300 days of sunshine per year and palm trees galore.

R.S. Hunter and his wife Kerry are dedicated Christians. He dedicates his writing to Kerry, to his stepsons Nicholas and Justin and their families including his grandchildren Daisy, Brandon, Jared, and Landon. His brothers David and Kevan and his sister Susan still live in Canada. His mother and father now walk with Jesus. R.S. Hunter feels he is truly blessed, so he gives thanks to God each and every day.

R.S. Hunter earned his Bachelor of Arts degree in mass communication, which has helped him fine-tune his writing skills. His first book, *Where Eagles Fly, Remember Me...*, tells the story of his father-in-law's experience as a WWII pilot and POW. His second book, *Will Work 4 Food*, brings the plight of Tucson's

232 homeless into light. It is a very sobering series of mini-biographies that will change how you view those most prefer to ignore. R.S. Hunter also wrote a children's story entitled *The Story Teller* which is posted on his website for all to read free of charge.

R.S. Hunter's mantra is from Proverbs 27:1:

Do not boast about tomorrow, for you do not know what a day may bring forth.

For more information about R.S. Hunter and his writings, please visit his website at **www.richardstevenhunter.com** and check out the Read4Free and Book Store tabs on the upper left corner.

In Memoriam: Pastor David Wilkerson

The strange white preacher from Pennsylvania (Chapter 2).

May 19, 1931 - April 27, 2011

Romans 14:8

For if we live, we live to the Lord;

and if we die, we die to the Lord.

Therefore, whether we live or die, we are the Lord's.

God Must Have Needed Another Angel

CPSIA information can be obtained at www.ICGtesting.com
Printed in the USA
BVOW080018290612

293845BV00007B/2/P